KU-171-709

★★★★ THE BEST ★★★★ FREE ATTRACTIONS IN THE SOUTHERN STATES

THE BEST ★★★★ FREE ATTRACTIONS

IN THE SOUTHERN STATES

by John Whitman

Meadowbrook Press

18318 Minnetonka Blvd. • Deephaven, MN 55391

*My thanks to all those people whose help and cooperation were essential in realizing **The Best Free Attractions:** Bert Berlowe, Greg Breining, Mary Cichy, Marcia Conley, Denise Hesselroth, Monty Mickelson, Mary Rockcastle, Amy Rood, Sue Veazie—and the thousands of people across the US who contributed their time and information so willingly.*   *J.W.*

First Printing April 1981

*All rights reserved. No part of this book may be reproduced in any form without permission from the publisher, except in the case of brief quotations embodied in critical articles and reviews. Information contained herein is subject to change without notice. Neither the publisher nor the author is responsible for any inconvenience, injury, damage or loss sustained by anyone visiting the attractions listed in **The Best Free Attractions.***

Printed in the United States of America
ISBN 0-915658-38-0
Copyright © 1981 by John Whitman

Editor: Kathe Grooms
Designer: Terry Dugan
Illustrator: John Shank
Production Manager: John Ware

CONTENTS

Free! That's the key. *The Best Free Attractions* is unlike any other travel guide you can find, because it lists hundreds of terrific travel attractions that don't cost a penny. You'll be amazed at what great things there are to do and see that are *still* free in this country.

You will find free zoos, aquaria and planetaria; hiking and biking trails; outdoor attractions like scenic wonders, parks, beaches and even free campsites; curiosities like ghost towns, reversible waterfalls, giant statues, UFO-sighting spots and folk art creations; wonderful festivals, fairs, plays, concerts and films; historic sites and museums; gardens, architectural sights and picnic spots; pro sports team practices, behind-the-scene tours and TV show tapings; plus parades, fireworks ... and more. There's something for everyone here!

Every entry in this book has been carefully evaluated and verified. Attractions that only let certain people in free (for example, kids or seniors) aren't listed—only those that are truly free for everybody. I've even found out when the free-entry days or periods fall for fee-charging attractions, and they're listed here as well.

The book is organized alphabetically by state and by towns within them. Each description is headed by the name of the nearest town. Attractions that are regional (like beaches) or scattered throughout the state (like free campsites) are listed in a separate category headed "Statewide." These listings follow the alphabetical town listings. When times are specified, they are for when the attraction is free (if no day is specified you can assume the hours apply seven days a week). The contact phone numbers and addresses are all accurate as we go to press, but be aware that they are changeable and call ahead if you're planning a special trip based on a single attraction. Also call ahead if you're planning a holiday excursion—holiday hours often differ from regular ones.

In these days of rising costs, you may find an attraction listed here as free which has begun to charge admission since we went to press. If you do find significant changes, please do let me know so I can change future listings and keep this book accurate. There's a page in the back of this book for your comments.

Take advantage of the free fun listed in this book. You'll experience an authentic slice of American life, unmarred by commercial hype. I hope you'll use *The Best Free Attractions* frequently ... and remember that good times *don't* have to be expensive!

ALABAMA

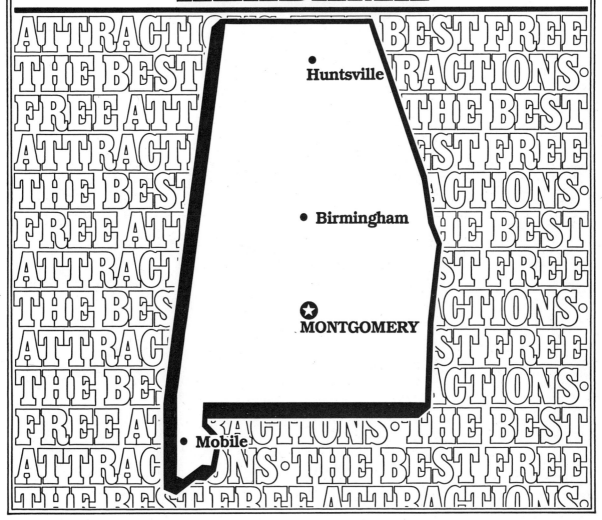

Huntsville

Birmingham

★ MONTGOMERY

Mobile

ALABAMA

Anniston

Stuffed Elephant

The Anniston Museum of Natural History has one of the largest collections of specimens in the US, including the popular African Hall with mounted animals. Over 280 species of North American birds have been preserved here, many of which are now extinct.

Time: Mem. Day-Labor Day, Mon.-Fri., 9 a.m.-5 p.m.; Sat., 10 a.m.-5 p.m.; Sun., 1-5 p.m. Rest of year, Tues.-Fri., 9 a.m.-5 p.m. (Tues. and Thurs., 9 a.m.-9 p.m.); Sat., 10 a.m.-5 p.m.; Sun., 1-5 p.m.
Place: 4301 McClellen Blvd.
Contact: (205) 237-6766

Gothic Shrine

The Church of St. Michael and All Angels, built in 1887, is one of the South's most lovely with its Carrara marble altar, intricate wood carvings and magnificent stained glass windows.
Time: 9 a.m.-4 p.m.
Place: 18th St. and Cobb Ave.
Contact: (205) 237-4011

Birmingham

Gardens

The Birmingham Botanical gardens cover 67 1/2 acres and include a 5,000-plant conservatory, a rose garden (with 125 varieties), an arboretum of rare shrubs and trees, and a 26-foot floral clock.
Time: Dawn to dusk.
Place: 2612 Lane Park Rd.
Contact: (205) 879-1227

Japanese Tea Ceremony

A Japanese Tea Ceremony is held several times each year at the Tea House in the Japanese Gardens. A stroll through these gardens is worthwhile at any time, taking you to goldfish ponds and across bridges that span flowing brooks.
Time: Tea Ceremony: 3rd Sun. of Mar., Apr. and May. Call for exact times.
Place: 2612 Lane Park Rd.
Contact: (205) 879-1227

Haunted Furnaces

The Sloss City Furnaces, built in 1882 by the Sloss-Sheffield Steel and Iron Company, now lie unused and rusting as a reminder of the industrial revolution. A phantom foundry man is said to appear frequently to workmen and guards in this area.
Place: First Ave., North Viaduct.

190 Million Years

The Red Mountain Museum features a cut through the earth that takes you through 190 million years of geologic time. The museum also features displays on Indians of Alabama, a cosmology section and a telescope which allows you to view activity on the sun's surface.
Time: Tues.-Sat., 10 a.m.-5 p.m.; Sun., noon-5 p.m.
Place: 1425 22nd St. S.
Contact: (205) 254-2757

Historic Pioneer Homes

There's usually a charge for a tour of the McAdory House and the Owen and Sadler Pioneer Homes. But during the Christmas tour you get to visit all three for free.
Time: 2nd weekend in Dec.
Place: Check with West Jefferson Historical Society for exact details.
Contact: (205) 426-6604

Antebellum Home

Arlington, the oldest home in the city (1822), has been fully restored and authentically furnished. Normally, there's a charge to see it. However, during the Arlington County Fair (blue grass music, clogging, arts and crafts) and Christmas at Arlington, you can enter this historic building free of charge.

Time: Arlington County Fair: mid-Sept. Christmas at Arlington: mid-Dec.
Place: 331 Cotton Ave. SW.
Contact: (205) 780-5656

Superb Wedgwood Collection

Part of the Kress Collection; Asian ceramics; paintings from the 17th to 19th centuries; and the outstanding Dwight and Lucille Beeson Wedgwood Collection, one of the finest in the world—these are all on hand at the Birmingham Museum of Art.

Time: Mon.-Sat., 10 a.m.-5 p.m. (Thurs., 10 a.m.-9 p.m.); Sun., 2-6 p.m.
Place: 2000 Eighth Ave.
Contact: (205) 254-2565

Bridgeport

Russell Cave

At this National Monument you'll find a cave in which Indians were building fires 3,000 years before the pyramids came into existence. The cave was inhabited by Stone Age men for 8,000 years. It's 26 feet high and 107 feet wide.

There's recorded information in one of the excavated pits.

Time: Mem. Day-Labor Day, 8 a.m.-6 p.m. Rest of year, 8 a.m.-5 p.m.
Place: 8 mi. W of town off US 72 via Cty. Rds. 91 and 75.
Contact: (205) 495-2672

Cherokee

Coon Dog Memorial Park

If you're a dog lover, this cemetery honoring beloved coon dogs will touch your heart. It's the only one of its kind in the world. And only super coon dogs are allowed to be buried here!

Place: From Tuscumbia W on Hwy. 72 for 7 mi., left on AL

247 for 12 mi., then follow signs.
Contact: (205) 360-2451

Dadeville

Indian Battle Recalled

At Horseshoe Bend National Military Park you can take a 3-mile auto tour of the Indian battle site where white settlers led by Andrew Jackson clashed with Creek Indians in 1814. There are 15 miles of hiking trails and a museum which explains the battle.

Time: Museum: 8 a.m.-4:30 p.m. Park: 8 a.m.-dusk.
Place: 12 mi. N of town on AL 49.
Contact: (205) 234-7111

Decatur

Mousetraps

Make a million with a new mousetrap! Take a look at the designs of the antique and modern mousetraps on display at Cook's Natural Science Museum, which also features 100 species of butterflies, live snakes (copperheads and rattlers) and a salt-water aquarium. And there are free movies to boot!

Time: Mon.-Sat., 9 a.m.-5 p.m. (closed for lunch); Sun., 2-5 p.m.
Place: 412 13th St. SE.
Contact: (205) 350-9347

ALABAMA

Decatur

Victorian Architecture

Pick up a free brochure from the Chamber of Commerce which will lead you to a section rich with fine Victorian homes and businesses. Don't miss the Old State Bank; Sherman, Jackson and Grant Streets; and the late Victorian residential district of Albany.
Time: Mon.-Fri., 9 a.m.-5 p.m.
Place: US 31 at Walnut St. NE.
Contact: (205) 353-5312

Enterprise

Boll Weevil Monument

This was the first monument ever erected to a pest—the boll weevil. The heroic act of the weevil was that it managed to destroy the cotton crops and so push Enterprise into a more profitable crop: peanuts. The town has been grateful ever since.
Place: The Square.

Peanut Butter Tour

Sessions Co. produces 800 cases of peanut butter an *hour.* You can see the whole process in a brief tour of the plant as long as there's one adult for every five kids.
Time: Mon.-Thurs., 8 a.m.-noon. But call 2 days ahead to reserve a place.
Place: 108 W. College.
Contact: (205) 347-9551, ext. 242

Eufaula

Antebellum Alabama

For the flavor of the Old South, drive past the many antebellum homes of Eufaula. Stop in at the Wellborn House for a look through its contemporary art museum.
Time: Mon.-Fri., 8 a.m.-5 p.m.
Contact: (205) 687-3879

Florence

TVA Dam

Wilson Dam, the largest of the TVA Dams, can be toured by appointment only. Tours include the locks, powerhouse and sometimes the tunnel.
Time: 9 a.m.-5 p.m., by appt.
Place: 5 mi E on US 72, 2 mi. S on AL 133.
Contact: (205) 386-2601

Ft. Payne

Little River Canyon

The drive through Little River Canyon takes you into one of the largest and deepest canyons east of the Rockies. The 400-to 600-foot cliffs box in the Little River, a turquoise ribbon surging and bubbling through boulder fields. You can take the 22-mile Canyon Rim Parkway (hairpin turns and steep grades) or hike the six-mile canyon trail.
Time: Best May-June when the mountain laurel blooms.
Place: I-59, DeSoto State Park area.
Contact: (205) 845-0051

DeSoto Falls

Here is an ideal picnic spot—pick one out near the 110-foot DeSoto Falls in the park that bears the same name.
Time: 8 a.m.-sunset.
Place: DeSoto State Park.
Contact: (205) 845-0051

Greensboro

Magnolia Grove

This is just one of the many antebellum homes in a town that was spared the torches of Union troops during the Civil War.
Time: Tues.-Sat., 10 a.m.-4 p.m.; Sun., 1-4 p.m.
Place: 1 Main St.
Contact: (205) 624-8618

Gulf Shores

Fort Morgan

"Damn the torpedos .... full speed ahead"—that was the

order of Admiral Farragut who braved the torpedos strung across Mobile Bay. His troops bombarded Fort Morgan with 3,000 cannon balls, forcing a surrender the next day. Numbered plaques lead you on a tour of this impressive, star-shaped brick bastion.
Time: Fort: 8 a.m.-sunset. Museum: June-Labor Day, 8 a.m.-5 p.m.; rest of year, 9 a.m.-5 p.m.
Place: 21 mi. W of town on AL 180.
Contact: (205) 540-7125

Huntsville

Free Concert
A special Pops-in-the-Park performance is given free of charge each year by the Huntsville symphony. If you're nearby in May, don't miss it.
Time: Mid-May, Sun.
Place: Big Spring Park.
Contact: Huntsville Symphony, P.O. Box 2340, Huntsville, AL 35804; (205) 539-4818.

Twickenham Historic Tour
For directions for one of Alabama's best historic home tours, pick up a free brochure from the Chamber of Commerce. It will lead you to the town's most beautiful and significant sights.
Time: Mon.-Sat., 9 a.m.-5 p.m.
Place: 700 Monroe St.
Contact: (205) 533-0125

Watercolors
The Burritt Museum, on a scenic mountaintop, is built in the shape of a Maltese cross. Surrounded by formal gardens, the converted home contains antique furnishings and a collection of watercolors with poems.
Time: May-Aug., Tues.-Sun., noon-6 p.m.; Sept.-Nov., noon-5 p.m.
Place: 3101 Burritt Drive.
Contact: (205) 536-2882

Malbis

Byzantine-Style Church
Malbis Greek Orthodox Church is adorned with mosaics, murals and Greek religious art. And it rests in a rural area in the midst of a Greek community.
Time: 9 a.m.-noon and 2-5 p.m.

Mobile

Azalea Trail Festival
The city of Mobile will be forever grateful to the French, who brought azaleas here in 1754. They bloom from late February to early April. Follow a marked 37-mile azalea trail (free map at the Chamber of Commerce) and enjoy concerts, plays, home tours, beauty pageants and other activities as well during the Azalea Trail Festival—many of these activities are also free!
Time: Festival: Mar.-Apr. Chamber: Mon.-Fri., 8 a.m.-5 p.m.
Place: 108 S. Claiborne St.
Contact: (208) 690-4064 or 433-6951

Coronation Costumes
In the Museum of the City of Mobile there's a collection of 18 Mardi Gras Queens' coronation costumes, Mobile historic exhibits, Boehm porcelain and a carriage house with eight carriages.
Time: Tues.-Sat., 10 a.m.-5 p.m.; Sun., 1-5 p.m.
Place: 355 Government St.
Contact: (205) 438-7569

Southern Furniture
The Fine Arts Museum of the South has an excellent collection of antique Southern furniture. During the first weekend in September there's a free arts and crafts fair held here as well.
Time: Tues.-Sat., 10 a.m.-5 p.m.; Sun., noon-5 p.m.

ALABAMA

Mobile

Place: Langen Park on Museum Dr.
Contact: (205) 342-4642

Vintage Cars

Most of the cars (not all) are for sale at Vintage Autos and Antiques, which constantly rotates its display of ten or so antique cars. There's no charge to look!
Time: Mon.-Fri., 8 a.m.-5:30 p.m.; Sat., 9 a.m.-1 p.m.
Place: 850 Government St.
Contact: (205) 432-2054

Creole Cottage

"Creole Cottage" is a style of architecture originating in Mo-bile in 1840 and unique to the area. A prime example is Carlen House, restored to orig-inal condition and furnished with period pieces. Clothes typ-ical of the era are displayed on mannequins.
Time: Tues.-Sat., 10 a.m.-5 p.m.; Sun., 1-5 p.m.
Place: Carlen St. at Willcox.
Contact: (205) 438-7468

Montgomery

American Art

The Montgomery Museum of Fine Arts has a strong collec-tion of early and modern Amer-ican paintings.
Time: Tues.-Sat., 10 a.m.-5 p.m. (Thurs., 10 a.m.-9 p.m.); Sun., 1-6 p.m.
Place: 440 S. McDonough St.
Contact: (205) 834-3490

Governor's Mansion

In the early 1900s, the Greek Revival design of the mid-1800s was imitated by many wealthy families. The Gover-nor's Mansion, with its Corin-thian columns, parquet floors and exquisite chandeliers, is a fine example of that period.
Time: Tues., 10 a.m.-12:30 p.m.; Thurs., 2-4 p.m.
Place: 1142 S. Perry St.
Contact: (205) 834-3022

A Good View

For one of the best views in Alabama, head to the McMon-nies Fountain (1885) and stroll past the many antebellum homes in the area.
Place: Court Sq.

Alabama State Capitol

Stand on the bronze star where Jefferson Davis himself stood to become president of the Confederacy. The Capitol building is one of the best ex-amples of Greek Revival archi-tecture in the US.
Time: 8 a.m.-5 p.m.
Place: Capitol Hill on Bainbridge Ave.
Contact: (205) 832-5510

Hundreds of Flags

Here's a salute to the world's one and only flag museum. Hundreds of them are always on display at the Tumbling Waters Museum of Flags!
Time: 10 a.m.-4 p.m.
Place: Adams and Perry Sts.
Contact: (205) 262-5335

Lurleen B. Wallace Film

Lurleen Wallace was Alabama's only woman governor, and you can see a nine-minute film on her life at the Lurleen B. Wal-lace Museum. The place also

has mementoes of her life, including the gowns she wore in office.
Time: 9 a.m.-5 p.m.
Place: 725 Monroe St.
Contact: (205) 832-6615

Confederate White House

The first White House of the Confederacy has been authentically restored with the original furnishings used by the Jefferson Davises during their short three-month stay.
Time: 8 a.m.-5 p.m. (closed for lunch, Sat.-Sun.)
Place: Washington and Union Sts.
Contact: (205) 832-5269

Hank Williams and History

The Archives and History Building has one of the most complete historical collections in Alabama, with fine arts and silver displays as well. Note too the Hank Williams exhibit.
Time: 8 a.m.-5 p.m.
Place: 624 Washington Ave.
Contact: (205) 832-6510

Easter Pageant

Christ's last days on earth are portrayed by a cast of 100 atop the Indian Mounds. The one-hour performance begins before sunrise to take advantage of the dramatic setting. Choir

and organ music add a special touch.
Time: Easter, 4:15 a.m.
Place: Moundville State Historic Site.
Contact: (205) 371-2641

Oneonta

Covered Bridge

There are 14 covered bridges in Alabama, but the best is Horton Mill Covered Bridge. It's 220 feet long and crosses the Black Warrior River at a height of 70 feet.
Contact: Inquire at Oneonta for specific directions.

Ozark

85 Helicopters

The US Army Aviation Museum at Fort Rucker has the world's best collection of helicopters and aircraft dating from 1942 to the present.
Time: Mon.-Fri., 10 a.m.-5 p.m.; Sat.-Sun., 1-5 p.m.
Place: 13 mi. SW of town on AL 85 at Ft. Rucker.
Contact: (205) 255-4507

Perdido

Wine Tasting

Perdido Vineyards Winery gives tours of its historic buildings and winery as well as free samples of its white table wines. It's the first farm winery established since Prohibition in this state.
Time: Mon.-Sat., 10 a.m.-5 p.m. Tours on the hour.
Place: I-65 at the Perdido-Rabun exit, near Bay Minette.
Contact: (205) 937-9463

Selma

Antebellum Business District

Walk along picturesque Water Avenue for a glimpse of one of the few antebellum business districts still intact.

ALABAMA

Selma

Historic Site

Ruins—that's all that's remaining of what was once Alabama's capital, a flourishing 19th-century town. Both floods and the Civil War have forced people to move out of this devastated area which was never able to recuperate.

Time: Sunrise to sunset.
Place: 9 mi. W of town on AL 22, then 4 mi. S.

Tuscaloosa

Southern Colonial Architecture

The Gorgas Home, once the dining hall of the University of Alabama, dates back to 1829 and is a picture-book example of Southern Colonial architecture. Inside are family mementoes and silver, some of which date back to 1680.

Time: Mon.-Sat., 10 a.m.-noon and 2-5 p.m.; Sun., 3-5 p.m.
Place: University of Alabama campus.
Contact: (205) 348-5906

Moody-Warner Home

Built in 1820, this home is a treasure of 17th- and 18th-century American antiques. It also displays a substantial collection of art from the Impressionist and Illuminist schools.

Time: By appt. only.
Contact: (205) 345-4062 or 553-6200

Superb Art Collection

In the National Headquarters of Gulf State Paper Corporation is an outstanding collection of sculpture, paintings and primitive artifacts—so good it should be on any art fancier's itinerary. There are peaceful walkways and Oriental gardens as well.

Time: Mon.-Fri., 5-8 p.m.; Sat., 10 a.m.-8 p.m.; Sun., 1:30-8 p.m.
Place: 1400 River Rd.
Contact: (205) 553-6200

Tuskegee

Carver Museum

Here you'll find the fully revamped George Washington Carver Museum, which outlines the careers of Carver as artist, teacher and scientist. In this latter role he's credited with developing more than 300 by-products of peanuts. His laboratory has been preserved, and there's a free film on his life.

Time: 9 a.m.-5 p.m.
Place: Tuskegee Institute campus.
Contact: (205) 727-6390

Statewide

Rubbings

In Alabama are dozens of Civil War vintage cemeteries where you can make rubbings of fascinating tombstones. Plain brown wrapping paper and charcoals or crayons are all it takes to come home with a bit of Alabama history.

Contact: (205) 832-5510

Coastal Drive

One of every ten Alabama travelers heads to the beach. US 98 offers an indirect but far more interesting route to the coast than does the more direct and faster AL 59. At Fairhope take *scenic* US 98 west and follow the shoreline of Mobile Bay for approximately ten miles. At Foley head south to Gulf Shores via AL 59.

Contact: (205) 832-5510

ARKANSAS

ATTRACTIONS·THE BEST FREE
THE BEST FREE ATTRACTIONS·
FREE
ATT
THE
• Jonesboro
FRE
ATT
THE
• Fort Smith
FRE
ATT
THE
ATT
THE
FRE
⭐ LITTLE ROCK
THE
ATT
THE
FRE
ATTRACTIONS·THE BEST FREE
THE BEST FREE ATTRACTIONS·

ARKANSAS

Altus

Wiederkehr Wine Cellars

Started a century ago and now encompassing 500 acres, this vineyard is known locally for its white, rosé and red wines. Visit the old cellars and sample three varieties of wines free of charge.

Time: Mon.-Sat., 9 a.m.-4:30 p.m.
Place: 2 mi. N of town on St. Mary's Mount, 3 mi. S of I-40, exit 41.
Contact: (501) 468-2611

Crossette

Timber Trail

At the Levi Wilcoxon Demonstration Forest, virgin timber has been preserved. A marked trail identifies local plants and trees. Pleasant family outing and hike!

Time: Sunrise to sunset.
Place: 15 mi. E of town at intersection of US 82 and AR 81.
Contact: (501) 567-8111

Dardanelle

Bridge Rock Trail

A one-mile trail offers three different routes of varying degrees of challenge. Wind along the wooded shoreline of Shoal Bay Park which borders Lake Dardanelle.

Time: Sunrise to sunset.
Place: 20 mi W of Dardanelle.
Contact: (501) 378-5551

Fort Smith

Old Fort River Festival

The historic Riverfront is jammed during this three-day event attracting 50,000 people each May. Over 300 musicians give 27 performances. And there are displays by artists and artisans. A major event!

Time: May. Call for exact times and dates of events.
Place: Ft. Smith Riverfront.
Contact: (501) 452-7278

National Historic Site

Both Fort Smith and Van Buren across the river have dozens of notable historic buildings—don't miss the Belgrove Historic District! This National Historic Site features barracks, "Hanging Judge" Parker's courtroom, a jail and a gallows. A film gives background on the colorful town, which witnessed the hanging of 79 felons in a 21-year period.

Time: 8:30 a.m.-5 p.m.
Place: Rogers Ave., between Second and Third Sts.
Contact: (501) 783-3961

Gillett

Pioneer Homestead

The Arkansas Post County Museum is a recreated pioneer homestead of the 1800s with exhibits from that era. You'll find also a smokehouse, a dog-trot log cabin, gallows and a three-room playhouse.

Time: Tues.-Sat., 9 a.m.-4:30 p.m.; Sun., 1-4:30 p.m.
Place: 5 mi. S of town via AR 169, at jct. AR 1.
Contact: (501) 548-2634

Harrison

Popular Canoe Route

The Buffalo River, a part of the National River System, is extremely well-known among canoeists who camp on its numerous sandbars. Less well-known but very fine is Cossatot River, southeast of Mena. It appeals to more experienced canoeists who want to avoid the crowds.

Contact: Buffalo National River, P.O. Box 1173, Harrison, AR 72601; (501) 741-5443.

Havana

State's Highest Point

Here's one of the best views in the state. Climb to the top of Mount Magazine, which rises

2,735 feet above the Arkansas River Valley. There are picnic areas and developed trails for hikers.

Place: Off AR 309, E of town.
Contact: (501) 963-2072

Heber Springs

Greers Ferry Water Festival

As a thank-you to all visitors, the US Army Corps of Engineers and the Regional Tourist Association sponsor free food, entertainment and hot air balloon races at Greer Ferry Lake each August.

Time: In Aug. Call contact for exact dates.
Contact: (501) 378-5551

Greers Ferry Lake Trails

Mossy Bluff Trail, Buckeye Trail and Sugar Loaf Mountain Trail all provide panoramic views of the lake below. There are special routes for handicapped people. For more information write to the contact below.

Contact: Little Rock District Corps of Engineers, P.O. Box 867, Little Rock, AR 72201; (501) 378-5551.

Hindsville

Ozark Arts and Crafts Fair

This fair attracts 350 artists and artisans from the four-state Ozark region who are allowed to sell only authentic hand-crafted goods typical of the area. In this idyllic rural setting 150,000 people congregate each October to enjoy the displays set up in four huge circus tents.

Time: 3rd weekend in Oct.
Place: War Eagle Mills Farm, 10 mi E of town—ask locally for exact directions.
Contact: (501) 789-5398

Hope

Watermelon Festival

"Home of the World's Largest Watermelons," Hope's largest on record was a 200-pound monster produced in 1979. In honor of its hefty cash crop the city hosts a festival in August.

Time: Late Aug. Call contact for exact dates.
Contact: (501) 777-3640

Jonquils in Bloom

In Old Washington Historical State Park thousands of jonquils bloom in mid-March, carpeting the land in yellow and gold—cause for a local Jonquil Festival. Both entry into the park and admission to the festival are free, but there is a charge to visit the restored buildings, once the Confederate Capitol from 1863 to 1865.

Time: Jonquil Festival: mid-Mar. Park: sunrise-sunset.
Place: 8 mi. NW of town off I-30 on AR 4.
Contact: (501) 983-2684

Hot Springs

Healing Springs

When Europeans arrived here in 1541, they found Indians already taking advantage of the area's hot springs, now a national park. These 47 springs produce a million gallons of steaming water daily.

ARKANSAS

Hot Springs

Visit the two open springs and be sure to see historic Bathhouse Row, bordered by magnolias. Don't miss the film at the visitor center, explaining both the history and geology of the area. Although there's a charge for baths, the park, known for its 23 miles of wooded trails, is free.

Time: Visitor center: June-Aug., 8 a.m.-7 p.m.; rest of year, 8 a.m.-5 p.m.
Place: Central and Reserve Aves.
Contact: (501) 624-3383

Scenic Drive

It's not as well-known as the Talimena Scenic Drive, but AR 7, running from Hot Springs north to Harrison, takes you through some of the state's most memorable terrain and comes highly recommended!

Little Rock

MacArthur's Birthplace

MacArthur was born in the building that is now the city's Museum of Science and History. Rotating exhibits which include multi-media presenta-tions portray facets of Arkansas and its people.

Time: Mon.-Sat., 9 a.m.-5 p.m.; Sun., 1-5 p.m.
Place: MacArthur Park.
Contact: (501) 376-4321

Ouachita Hiking Trail

The Ouachita Trail runs for 175 miles from Lake Sylvia near Little Rock to Oklahoma. Different segments offer easy-to-difficult hikes, which vary from 2 to 17 miles and longer. Write the contact below for more information.

Contact: Forest Supervisor, Ouachita National Forest, Hot Springs, AR 71901; (501) 623-7763.

Riverfest

A joyous four-day festival with mostly free events including performances by nationally-known musicians and the Arkansas Symphony Orchestra. Hot air balloon races, ethnic foods, 16 kid-oriented booths and gigantic fireworks add to the fun.

Time: Late May. Call contact for exact times of events.
Place: Little Rock's Riverfront.
Contact: (501) 376-4781

Quapaw Quarter

This three-mile square in downtown Little Rock includes historic structures from ante-bellum homes to Victorian mansions—all easy to see on a walking tour.

Contact: Quapaw Quarter Assn., P.O. Box 1104, Little Rock, AR 72203; (501) 371-0075.

State Capitol

Artwork and historic exhibits are displayed in this impressive building with its six brass doors designed by Tiffany in New York.

Time: Mon.-Fri., 7:30 a.m.-6 p.m.; Sat.-Sun., 1-5 p.m.
Place: W end of Capitol Ave.
Contact: (501) 371-3000

The Old State House

This Greek Revival building, completed in 1836 for the first session of the Arkansas State Legislature, can be seen on regularly scheduled guided tours. Tours also include the Museum of State History, noted for its collection of gowns worn by Arkansas's first ladies.

Time: Mon.-Sat., 9 a.m.-4 p.m.; Sun., 1-5 p.m.
Place: 300 W. Markham St.
Contact: (501) 371-1749

Arkansas Art Center

One of the state's best—fine paintings, sculptures and ceramics are featured in a series of five galleries.

Time: Mon.-Sat., 10 a.m.-5 p.m.; Sun., noon-5 p.m.
Place: MacArthur Park.
Contacts: (501) 372-4000

McNeil

Ecology Games

Wild orchids, springs, slide programs, films and ecology games—all are offered in the state's first environmental education park, which includes trails through a Gulf Coastal Plain forest.

Time: Sunrise to sunset.
Place: Logoly State Park, 1.5 mi. E of town, .75 mi. E of US 79.
Contact: (501) 695-3561

Mena

Talimena Scenic Drive

This is Arkansas's and Oklahoma's best-known scenic route. Take advantage of the area's natural beauty—follow AR 88 and then OK 1 through part of the Ouachita National Forest. Stop at Wilhelmina State Park for the view from Rich Mountain.

Time: Best in early spring and fall.

Janssen Park

Janssen Park, ten acres in all, has spring-fed lakes and a deer herd. Wonderful spot for a picnic.

Place: Janssen and Seventh Sts.
Contact: (501) 394-2912

Morrilton

Petit Jean State Park

This is one of the oldest and best state parks in Arkansas with an excellent view from the lodge. The Seven Hollows Trail (a four-hour hike) and Cedar Creek Trail (suited to families and leading to 70-foot Cedar Falls) are both enjoyable, depending upon your hiking skill.

Place: 17 mi. SW of town via AR 9 and 154.
Contact: (501) 727-5441

Mountain View

Hootenany

For authentic Ozark fiddling and banjo pickin', head to the Rackensack Folk Musicals outside the local courthouse on Friday evenings.

Time: Fri. evening.
Place: Courthouse.
Contact: (501) 269-3271

Pea Ridge

National Military Park

A slide presentation gives background information on the bloody battle which took place here on March 7-8, 1862, resulting in the death of three Confederate generals.

Time: June-Aug., 8 a.m.-6 p.m.; rest of year, 8 a.m.-5 p.m.
Place: Off US 62, N of Rogers and 10 mi. SE of Pea Ridge.
Contact: (501) 451-8122

Ponca

Lost Valley Trail

The Lost Valley Trail is dwarfed by steep cliffs as it follows Clark Creek. Watch the water emerge from a cave and tumble at your feet—picturesque and beautiful.

Place: S of town on AR 74.
Contact: (501) 365-5443

ARKANSAS

Prairie Grove

Battlefield Reenactment

Every two years troops clash in Prairie Grove Battlefield State Park as they reenact a Civil War skirmish that took place in 1862. It's a big and colorful event worth seeking out.

Time: Lake Oct. in even-numbered years. Lack of funds may force this event to be canceled—please call.
Place: SW of Fayetteville on US 62.
Contact: (501) 846-2990

Rogers

Non-Powder Gun Collection

The Daisy International Air Gun Museum has the finest collection of non-powder guns in the world! It includes hundreds of models dating back to 1896.

Time: Mon.-Fri., 8 a.m.-5 p.m.
Place: 1 mi. S of town on US 71.
Contact: (501) 636-1200

Roland

Bald Eagles

Bald eagles congregate in Pinnacle Mountain State Park every January. The climb to the top of the 1,011-foot mountain affords an eagle's eye view of the surrounding region.

Place: 12 mi. W of Little Rock via AR 10 to Cty. Farm Rd. Turn off on Pinnacle Valley Rd.
Contact: (501) 868-5806

Stuttgart

Prairie Lifestyle

The Arkansas County Agricultural Museum shows how the prairie farmer worked, lived and played. There's even a 30-minute slide show on rice farming in the area.

Time: Tues.-Sat., 10 a.m.-4 p.m. (closed during lunch); Sun., 1:30-4:30 p.m.
Place: 921 E. Fourth St.
Contact: (501) 673-7001

Duck-Calling Contest

When someone says "duck" in Stuttgart, watch out for a mallard. Renditions of this bird's "feed" and "comeback" calls separate world champions from poor imitation quackers in one of the all-time zaniest and most amusing competitions in the country—the world championship duck-calling contest!

Time: Thanksgiving weekend.
Place: Main St. (Quackers hide behind screens.)
Contact: (501) 673-1602

Rice Packaging Plant

Rice is big business in the Stuttgart area. Ricelands Foods opens its doors to visitors by appointment only and will show a 20-minute slide presentation when pressed. Worth it, if you're in the area.

Time: By appt.
Place: First and Coledge Sts.
Contact: (501) 673-5500

Weiner

Arkansas Rice Festival

In the rice bowl of the country you'd expect a rice festival with no less than 200 dishes to sample. Here it is with free entertainment added.

Time: Oct., but call for exact date.
Place: Off AR 49.
Contact: (501) 684-2244

Wilson

Indian Artifacts

The Hampson Museum State Park exhibits artifacts of Mound Builder Indians. Ceramics (note the human head effigy vessel), distinctive red and white pottery, and stone tools are on display.

Time: Mon.-Sat., 9 a.m.-5 p.m.; Sun., 1-5 p.m.
Place: N edge of town on US 61.
Contact: (501) 655-8622

Winslow

Explore the Devil's Den

Take a mile and a half woodland path to a four-foot wide, 186-yard deep fracture in a steep sandstone wall. Bring a lantern to explore this chilly, eerie cave known locally as the "Devil's Den." Butterfield Hiking Trail, a full 14½-mile hike, will appeal to serious backpackers. Don't forget to pick up a free hiking permit before heading out into the wilderness.

Place: 13 mi. W of town on AR 74.
Contact: (501) 761-3325

Yellville

Ozark Folk Music

At Buffalo Point local musicians entertain campers throughout the summer in evening performances. An excellent network of trails lead to caves, old homesteads and clear springs.

Place: Buffalo Point, 17 mi. S of town via AR 14 and 268.
Contact: (501) 449-6206

FLORIDA

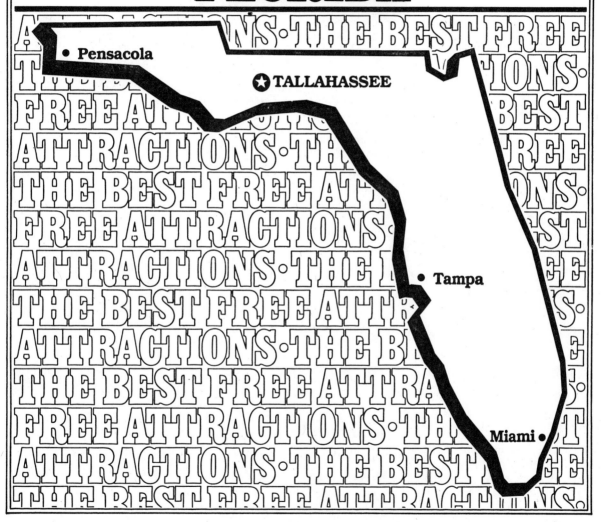

- Pensacola
- ★ TALLAHASSEE
- Tampa
- Miami

FLORIDA

Apopka

House Plant Haven

Apopka is a small town with many nurseries that grow house plants. In fact, there are so many nurseries growing so many house plants that this town supplies most of the greenery that Florida produces. Many such firms conduct informal tours. Phone or stop in at the contact below for a free travel guide that lists area nurseries.

Time: Anytime.
Place: All over town.
Contact: Florida Foliage Assn., 116 E. Fifth St., Apopka, FL 32703; (305) 886-1036.

Arcadia

Cattle Auctions

Calves, cows and bulls are delivered every week to the Arcadia State Livestock Market. Come in and watch the excitement as the auctioneers put these animals up for bids. But think twice before you tip your hat—you might go home with a bull!

Time: Wed., 1 p.m.
Place: 1 mi. N of town on US 17.
Contact: (813) 494-1808

Big Pine Key

Dog-size Deer

A variety of white-tailed deer the size of German shepherds, alligators, crocodiles, bald eagles, white ibis, egrets and a variety of other wildlife are the main attractions of the refuge on Big Pine Key.

Time: Visitor center: Mon.-Fri. 8 a.m.-5 p.m.
Place: Watson Blvd., 5 mi. N of US 1.
Contact: (305) 872-2239

Bradenton

De Soto Memorial

Crossbow demonstrations are part of the attractions at the De Soto National Memorial. The memorial marks the approximate site where Hernando de Soto landed in 1539 with 600 conquistadores and began his conquest of the New World.

Time: 8 a.m.-5:30 p.m.
Place: 5 mi. W on FL 64, then 2 mi. N on 75th St. W.
Contact: (813) 792-0458

Brooksville

Rogers Christmas House

This specially constructed village has five buildings, each with a different theme. The Rogers Christmas House, with 10 rooms, is decorated in keeping with the nearest holiday. Another building, Storybook Land, is a treat for children. Exhibits there represent Dickens characters or scenes from fairy tales.

Time: Mon.-Sat., 9:30 a.m.-5 p.m.; Sun., 10:30 a.m.-5 p.m.
Place: 103 Saxon Ave.
Contact: (904) 796-2415

Caryville

Fiddling for Worms

By plunging a wooden stake into the ground and drawing a heavy metal bar across it, you can set up vibrations that attract earthworms to the surface. Of course, someone made a sport of it, and that is the basis of the International Worm-Fiddling Contest. Watch men, women and children compete in their respective divisions, all of them trying to catch the most and the longest worms. Then it's time to eat—not worms, but fish.

Time: Sat. before Labor Day.
Place: Ask directions locally.
Contact: (904) 547-2270

Cedar Key

Fishing Village

Cross a series of bridges with scenic overlooks over the Gulf of Mexico to reach this quiet fishing village. Located on an island off the coast of Florida, Cedar Key was settled in 1884 and still retains much of its original quaint character.

Time: Anytime.
Place: On FL 24.
Contact: (904) 543-5410

Cocoa Beach

Cape Canaveral Tour

You can take a drive-through tour of Cape Canaveral Air Force Station and Kennedy Space Center on Sundays. There is a museum in the base with films on space exploration.

Time: Sun., 9 a.m.-3 p.m.
Place: Take FL A1A N of Cocoa Beach; exit into base.
Contact: (305) 494-7731

Missile Watch

Each year, NASA publishes a list of scheduled launches from Kennedy Space Center. Once you get that, you are ready to watch missiles blast off. Park along the beach or near Jetty Park and turn your radio to AM-1060 to listen to the countdown.

Time: Varies widely.
Place: Follow FL A1A N from Cocoa Beach and then take Jetty Park exit.
Contact: (305) 432-2153 (toll free only in Florida: 800-432-2153).

Surfing

The best surfing on Cocoa Beach is near the Canaveral Pier. The quality of the waves varies from day to day but the surfing is always free. You may have to pay for parking.

Time: Anytime.
Place: N on Meade Ave. to ocean.
Contact: (305) 636-4262

Daytona Beach

Giant Ground Sloth

The Cuban Foundation Collection at the Museum of Arts and Sciences includes paintings from the 18th through 20th centuries, lithographs, photos and ceramics. There also is the mounted skeleton of an Ice Age giant ground sloth.

Time: Free Wed., 1-5 p.m.
Place: 1040 Museum Rd.
Contact: (904) 255-0285

Del Ray Beach

Wildlife Refuge

When you walk the marsh trail through the Loxahatchee National Wildlife Refuge, hold on to your children! Not only are there sandhill cranes, herons, egrets and turtles; there are also alligators and they may be hungry! If you don't want to worry about the big reptiles, view them from an observation tower that's located directly across from the management area.

Time: Dawn to dusk.
Place: 3 mi. N of town via FL 806.
Contact: (305) 732-3684

Japanese Culture

The Morikami Museum of Japanese Culture and its 140-acre grounds include Japanese gardens with bonsai trees and exhibits of folk arts from

FLORIDA

Del Ray Beach

Japan. You must take off your shoes to enter the building.
Time: Tues.-Sun., 10 a.m.-5 p.m.
Place: 4 mi. W of I-90; take Linton Blvd. to Carter Rd., go S to Morikami Park Rd.
Contact: (305) 499-0631

Dundee

Candy and Fruit

Get free samples of fruit and candy on a tour of Davidson of Dundee, a company that makes candy from citrus fruits. The firm uses oranges, grapefruits and others, depending on the season.
Time: Mon.-Fri., 8 a.m.-5 p.m.
Place: 2 blocks N of FL 542 on US 27.
Contact: (813) 439-2284

Ensley

Weapons and Relics

If you have a real fascination for rifles, handguns, swords, coins, Indian artifacts, antique pianos and old caskets, you're sure to enjoy the T. T. Wentworth Jr. Museum. It has a wide variety of antique weapons and other materials of interest.
Time: Sat.-Sun., 2-5 p.m.
Place: 381 N. Palafox Hwy.
Contact: (904) 476-3443

Fernandina Beach

Historic Tavern

Stop in to see the Victorian surroundings of the Palace Saloon, Florida's oldest bar. The bar (and patrons who have visited it for too long) are supported by two wooden replicas of Greek goddesses. The bar and furnishings are made of carved oak and mahogany. This has been the hangout of the vacationing rich, including the Carnegies, Goodyears, Rockerfellers and Morgans.
Time: Mon.-Sat., 8 a.m.-2 a.m.
Place: 117 Century St.
Contact: (904) 261-3688

Fort Lauderdale

Harbor Tours

By calling ahead, you can arrange a tour of Florida's deepest port and one of its busiest. As you see the harbor in action, a Port Authority guide explains how the ships, cranes and petroleum pumps work together to deliver products both to overseas markets and to this country.
Time: Wed., 2:30 p.m.
Place: SE 24th St.
Contact: (305) 523-3404

Fort Myers

Thousands of Shells

Visit the Shell Factory, which claims to have one of the world's largest collections of seashells and coral. You can watch the shells being cleaned, polished and fashioned into lamps, ashtrays and other items. There's also a leather shop, two aquaria and a resident glass blower.
Time: 8 a.m.-7 p.m.
Place: 10 mi. N of town via US 41.
Contact: (813) 995-2141

Fort Pierce

Surfcasting

Twenty-one miles of the beach near Fort Pierce are open to surfcasters who want to try their luck at salt-water fishing from shore. There are free fishing balconies over the Indian River, where the world's record sea trout was caught. You're also able to fish in the fresh water of the nearby St. Lucie River. Write or call the contact below for information.
Time: Anytime.
Contact: Fort Pierce Chamber of Commerce, 2200 Virginia Ave., Fort Pierce, FL 33450; (305) 461-2700.

Gainesville

Mayan Art

Mayan and other ancient art is on display at the University of Florida Art Gallery. Contemporary paintings and sculpture also highlight the permanent exhibits.

Time: Mon.-Fri., 9 a.m.-5 p.m.; Sun. 1-5 p.m.
Place: SW 13th St. and Fourth Ave.
Contact: (904) 392-0201

Mayan Palace

The Mayan Palace at the Florida State Museum on the University of Florida campus is a reproduction of a village that may date back to Mexico 1,000 years ago. The collection includes sculptures, carved limestone tablets and a mural that covers the walls and ceiling of one entire room. Nearly 100 manikins are dressed in replicas of Mayan ceremonial headdresses, jewels and robes.

Time: Mon.-Sat., 9 a.m.-5 p.m.; Sun., 1-5 p.m.
Place: Museum Rd. near University Ave. and US 441.
Contact: (904) 392-1721

Morningside Nature Center

Just what you want to do on a vacation—go to work on a farm! But if that does appeal to you, come to the Morningside Nature Center, which is designed to give you the experience of working on a farm. You can milk a cow, gather eggs or make butter. There are also nature programs with lectures and walks. During the Sunday insect clinics, an entomologist will help you identify any insect you bring or find on the premises.

Time: Tues.-Sat., 8 a.m.-6 p.m.; Sun., noon-6 p.m. Insect clinic: Sun., 1:30-4 p.m.
Place: E. University Ave. at city limits.
Contact: (904) 374-2170

Hollywood

Jazz, Dance and Movies

Folk music, jazz, movies and dancing are among the Monday night activities at the Hollywood Beach Theater Under the Stars. Call ahead to ask about the specific event scheduled each week; in the summer, there may be additional concerts scheduled on Thursdays.

Time: Mon., 8 p.m.
Place: Johnson St. and the Boardwalk.
Contact: (305) 921-3404

Homestead

Biscayne National Park

This 103,701-acre preserve along the Florida coast is largely covered by water. Among the preserve's keys and coral reefs you'll find prime marine habitat. Camping is allowed only on Elliot Key, and you must have a boat to reach it. You can get more information by writing to the park.

Time: 8 a.m.-4:30 p.m.
Place: 9 mi. E of town on North Canal Dr.
Contact: Biscayne National Park, P.O. Box 1369, Homestead, FL 33030; (305) 247-2044.

Fruit and Spice

The 20 acres of the Redland Preston B. Bird and Mary Heinlein Fruit and Spice Park grow a variety of exotic trees and plants that produce spices, fruits and nuts. There are more than 350 varieties from 50 countries.

Time: Mon.-Sat., 8 a.m.-4:30 p.m.; Sun., 9 a.m.-5 p.m. Tours: Wed., 10:30 a.m.; Sun., 1 and 3:30 p.m.
Place: N of Homestead on FL 27 at Coconut Palm Dr. and Redland Rd.
Contact: (305) 247-3743

FLORIDA

Homestead

Everglades

The Pinelands Primitive Auto Trail winds through the tropical, swampy, alligator-filled

Everglades National Park. The road leads to several interesting areas for side trips, including a 17-mile loop through Shark Valley where only bikers and hikers can venture. Besides alligators, turtles and snakes, there are 240 species of birds. The waterways in the park can be traveled by canoe. One visitor center has a free 17-minute film and a slide show; another center plays a recording of night sounds.

Time: Anytime. Visitor centers: 8 a.m.-5 p.m.
Place: 12 mi. S of town via Rte. 27.
Contact: Everglades National Park, P.O. Box 279, Homestead, FL 33030; (305) 247-6211.

Jackson

Shipyard View

From the observation balcony on the 19th floor of the Prudential Insurance Company office, Florida's tallest building, you can see the Jackson shipyards and the St. Johns River. You also can learn about the insurance business during the rest of the tour. Be sure to call ahead and make an appointment.

Time: Mon.-Fri., 10:30 a.m., 3 p.m., by appt. only.
Place: 841 Prudential Dr.
Contact: (904) 399-2711

Jacksonville

Old French Fort

Fort Caroline, built by the French in 1564, was both the base for French raids against nearby Spanish encampments and the target of Spanish counter-attacks. A replica of this fort has been built on the banks of the St. Johns River.

Time: 8:30 a.m.-5 p.m.
Place: 12713 Ft. Caroline Rd., 10 mi. E of town on FL 10.
Contact: (904) 641-7155

Jensen Beach

Turtle Watch

During late spring or early summer, sea turtles weighing up to 500 pounds waddle onto Jensen Beach, scoop out their nests in the sand and begin laying eggs. Sometimes no turtles can be seen; at other times, there are many. Be patient and keep a sharp look-out.

Time: Usually in early June.
Place: Along the beach.
Contact: (305) 334-3444

Jupiter

To the Lighthouse

Tour one of the oldest lighthouses on the Atlantic Coast at the site of Fort Jupiter, built in 1838. There is a museum that displays old pictures of the lighthouse and guns used in battles with Indians of the area.

Time: Sun., noon-2:30 p.m.
Place: On the Jupiter Inlet.
Contact: (305) 746-3181

Wilderness Preserve

The Audubon Society has purchased and preserved the 120-acre Joseph Reed Sanctuary on Jupiter Island. The site, a large bird sanctuary, also is marked by historic Indian shell mounds. You can reach it by boat or by a 2 1/2-mile hike from the north end of Beach Road in Hope Sound.
Time: Dawn to dusk.
Place: Jupiter Island.
Contact: (305) 746-7111

Kissimmee

Livestock Auction

For more than 100 years, auctioneers have called out the fate of the cows, calves and bulls at the Kissimmee Livestock Auction. You're invited to come out and see how it's done.
Time: Wed. mornings.
Place: N edge of town near Old Dixie Hwy.
Contact: (305) 846-4181 or 847-3521

Monument of the States

This 100-foot-tall monument devoted to all states in the continental United States was built in the 1940s. It's constructed of concrete and all the trinkets that tourists contrib-uted at the time it was being assembled.
Time: Anytime.
Place: Monument St.
Contact: (305) 847-3174

Tupperware Headquarters

Come to Kissimmee and find out who is behind all those Tupperware parties. The company headquarters offers tours of a museum displaying historic containers (the oldest piece dates from 4000 B.C.), demonstrations in a model kitchen and strolls through a tropical garden.
Time: Mon.-Fri., 9 a.m.-4 p.m.
Place: 2.5 mi. N of town on US 441.
Contact: (305) 847-3111

Lake City

Tobacco Auction

Whenever farmers bring in their tobacco for sale, there is frantic activity at the warehouses in Lake City. Watch as buyers follow chanting auctioneers up and down the rows of tobacco.
Time: Usually in July and Aug.
Place: Washington and Seventh Sts.
Contact: (904) 752-3690

Lake Placid

Pineapples Galore

This pineapple plantation welcomes you to come and see how the fruit is grown. On days the workers are making preserves, you can also see that process. The area behind the plantation's main building offers an excellent view of the fields.
Time: 8 a.m.-6 p.m.
Place: 4 mi. S of town on US 27.
Contact: (813) 465-3760

Lake Wales

Ghosts on the Road

If you care to dabble with the unexplained, drive down to the bottom of Spook Hill, a steep hill on Fifth Avenue. (There is a marker there to show the spot.) After you turn the engine off and put it in neutral, your car will move backwards at least 100 feet, just as though it is being drawn back up the hill.
Time: Anytime.
Place: The foot of Fifth Ave.
Contact: (813) 676-3445

Nature Trail

You can walk along a 1 1/2-mile nature trail that winds through the woods on Crooked Lake. An Audubon Society

FLORIDA

Lake Wales

exhibit room just off the lake displays some of the area's wildlife.

Time: Nature trail: Dawn to dusk. Exhibit room: Nov.-May, Mon.-Sat., 9 a.m.-5 p.m., Sun., 1-5 p.m. June-Oct., call ahead for exact hours.
Place: 7 mi. S of town on US 27A in Babson Park.
Contact: (813) 638-1355

Singing Tower

Each day at 3 p.m. a carillon chimes from a 205-foot Bok Singing Tower in the Bok Tower Gardens. Swans swim the lagoons in this 100-acre tropical garden.

Time: Gardens: 8:30 a.m.-5:30 p.m. Carillon: 3 p.m.
Place: 3 mi. N of town on Burns Ave.
Contact: (813) 676-1408
Note: Though admission is free, there is a charge for parking.

Longwood

Big Old Tree

The Senator, the oldest and largest giant cypress in the country, sits in a park-like setting near Longwood. The tree is 126 feet tall, 17-1/2 feet in diameter and 47 feet around. It is about 3,500 years old.

Time: Anytime.
Place: Between Sanford and Longwood, just W of US 17-92.
Contact: (305) 322-2212

Mayport

Big Ships

See aircraft carriers, cruisers and destroyers during tours of the US Naval Station on Florida's Atlantic coast. You can drive around and view several ships or actually board one of the vessels.

Time: Sat., 10 a.m.-4 p.m.; Sun., 1-4 p.m.
Place: Mayport Rd.
Contact: (904) 246-5226 or 246-5440

Merritt Island

Kennedy Space Center

In the visitor center at Kennedy Space Center, you can see movies and exhibits about modern exploits in space. Although there is a charge for an organized tour, you can take a self-guided tour through the center for free. There are several models of Mercury and Gemini capsules on display, along with Saturn and Mercury Redstone rockets. Free lectures are also given at the visitor center.

Time: 8 a.m.-6 p.m.
Place: W edge of Kennedy Space Center on NASA Causeway.
Contact: (305) 452-2121

Miami

Cuban Tile

You are given a free sample when you tour the Tropic Cuban Tile Co. Here skilled workers decorate their wares by hand.

Time: Mon.-Fri., 9 a.m.-3 p.m.
Place: 3632 NW 37th Ave.
Contact: (305) 633-8941

Metropolitan Museum of Art

The Miami Metropolitan Museum of Art has six galleries, including extensive collections of Latin American, Oriental and pre-Columbian art. On the first floor of the museum, located in the old Biltmore Country Club, is an art school that can be toured by visitors.

Time: Free only on Wed., 10 a.m.-5 p.m., 7-10 p.m.
Place: 1212 Anastasia Ave.
Contact: (305) 442-1448

Japanese Tea House

Visit a replica of a Japanese Tea House and stroll through a Japanese garden. Though you can't have tea in the Japanese-style, two-room building, you can see bonsai trees, bamboo, a brook, a bridge and two pagodas in the garden.
Time: 9 a.m.-3:10 p.m.
Place: Watson Park near McArthur Causeway.
Contact: (305) 579-6944

Lowe Art Museum

The guides at the Lowe Art Museum tailor their tours to the visitors' ages and interests. Even the lengths of tours vary. Main-gallery shows are usually changed every six weeks.
Time: Tues.-Fri., noon-5 p.m.; Sat., 10 a.m.-5 p.m.; Sun., 2-5 p.m.
Place: 1301 Stanford Dr. on University of Miami campus.
Contact: (305) 284-3535

Miami Beach

Tropical Plants

Two hundred varieties of lush tropical plants are on display at the Miami Beach Garden Center and Conservatory. There are special displays on Easter and Christmas. A craft shop is open to the public.
Time: 10 a.m.-3:30 p.m.
Place: 2000 Convention Center Dr.
Contact: (305) 672-1270

Monticello

Free Watermelon

One of the benefits of attending the Jefferson County Watermelon Festival is free slices of watermelon. But there's more: watermelon eating and seed-spitting contests, an arts and crafts show, a horse show, country-western music and square dancing.
Time: Late June.
Place: Downtown.
Contact: (904) 997-5552

New Smyrna Beach

Mill Ruins

At the New Smyrna Sugar Mill Ruins State Historic Site are the remains of a large mill that was destroyed by the Seminoles. The walking beam from a steam locomotive and cooking pots remain. Nature trails criss-cross the site.
Time: 9 a.m.-noon, 1-5 p.m.
Place: 2 mi W of US 1 on FL 44.
Contact: (904) 428-2126

Ocala

Horse Farm

The pastoral region around Ocala has become well-known as a breeding ground of thoroughbreds. The grassy hills and mild climate seem tailored to this industry. Bonnie Heath Farm is one of several farms that allow tours.
Time: 9 a.m.-4 p.m.
Place: 5 mi. W of town on FL 200.
Contact: (904) 237-2171

Pools for Horses

The Ocala Stud Farm, one of the many thoroughbred farms in the region, has a training track and a swimming pool for horses. It's open to the public.
Time: 7-10 a.m., 1-3 p.m.
Place: SW 27th Ave., 2 mi. W of FL 200.
Contact: (904) 237-2121

Okeechobee

Big Dairy

The MacArthur Jersey Dairy milks some 8,000 cows a day. You can take a 45-minute tour of the five milking barns as the employees work. Then you can visit the calf barn, and children can touch and play with

FLORIDA

Okeechobee

some of the 1,200 calves kept there. Call ahead if possible.
Time: Mon.-Fri., 8 a.m.-5 p.m.
Place: 12 mi. N of town on S. Hwy. 441.
Contact: (813) 763-4673 or 763-4719

Orlando

Race Track

When you go to Ben White Raceway, you can walk right through the barns, look at the horses and watch the track's four blacksmiths work. At the raceway are two 2-1/2-mile tracks and a one-mile track.
Time: Oct.-May, Mon.-Sat., 7-11 a.m.
Place: 1905 Lee Rd.
Contact: (305) 293-8721

Palatka

300,000 Ornamentals

More than 300,000 ornamental plants grace the 182-acre landscaped grounds of Ravine State Gardens. If you're fond of azaleas, you'll be in heaven: here you'll see over 100,000 of them in 50 varieties.
Time: 8 a.m.-sundown; best Feb.-March.
Place: Twigg St. off Moseley Ave., 1 mi. SE of town.
Contact: (904) 328-4366

Panama City

Junior Museum

A reconstructed log cabin with furnishings of olden times, a grist and cane mill and a nature trail on a walkway through a swamp: all the attractions here are designed to keep children entertained.
Time: Mon.-Sat., 9 a.m.-4 p.m.; Sun., 2-4 p.m.
Place: 1731 Jenks Ave.
Contact: (904) 785-8722 or 785-6274

Pensacola

Aviation Museum

About 75 full-size aircraft and more than 200 models—from the F6F Hellcat to the Skylab Module—are on display at the Naval Aviation Museum. Photos, paintings and other memorabilia span the time from 1914 to the present.
Time: 9 a.m.-5 p.m.
Place: Bldg. no. 3465 on Radford Blvd.
Contact: (904) 452-3604

Oldest Church

The Pensacola Historical Museum is housed in Florida's oldest church, the Old Christ Church. On display are exhibits that describe the local history, featuring a collection of fine glassware, antique dresses and archaeological finds.
Time: Mon.-Sat., 9 a.m.-4:30 p.m.
Place: 405 S. Adams St.
Contact: (904) 433-1559

Board an Aircraft Carrier

When the USS Lexington is in port, you can board it and step back in history. It was the first aircraft carrier to steam into Tokyo Bay after World War II. The tour takes you through the hangar bay and onto the flight deck; visitors are not allowed below. The *Lexington,* commissioned in 1943, also saw service in the major Pacific battles. It is 910 feet long, 183 feet wide and weighs 40,000 tons.

Time: 9 a.m.-3 p.m. when ship is in port.
Place: Pensacola Base, main gate on Navy Blvd.
Contact: Tour: (904) 452-2723; ship: (904) 452-3122.

Perry

Free Fish Fry

The free fish fry that follows the Chainsaw Championship in Perry qualifies as one of the largest feeds of its kind. More than 9,000 pounds of mullet are cooked up for the event.
Time: End of Oct.
Place: Hwy. 19S in Perry.
Contact: (904) 584-5366

Pompano Beach

Farmers Market

Representatives of every large grocery chain in the country show up for the farmers market at Pompano Beach. The market platform itself is 1,000 feet long, 140 feet wide and can hold from 150 to 200 trucks of vegetables a day.
Time: Daylight hours.
Place: Hammondville Rd.
Contact: (305) 946-6570

Port Orange

Sugar Mill Gardens

The long history of Sugar Mill Gardens is gauged by a gnarled oak tree that began growing more than 500 years ago. When the tree was small, Spanish priests built a mission nearby. When the tree was a century old, a steam-powered sugar mill was built on the site. When the tree was 400 years old, Confederate soldiers lay under its spreading branches, waiting for their sugar rations. The mission now lies in ruin; the mill has been restored; the mighty oak still lives. Crushed-shell paths lined by roses and azaleas guide you through the area.
Time: 9 a.m.-4 p.m.
Place: 1 mi. W of US 1 on Herbert St.
Contact: (904) 767-1735

St. Augustine

First Mission

The 200-foot stainless steel cross planted at the Mission of Nombre de Dios commemorates the Spaniards' establishment of Christianity in what became the United States. The mission, the first

in the country, includes Prince of Peace Church, Shrine of Our Lady of Leche, a statue of Father Lopez de Mendoza Grajales and a diorama showing the mission's beginnings.
Time: Anytime.
Place: 200 block of San Marco Ave.
Contact: (904) 829-5696

Oldest City

St. Augustine is the nation's oldest city and is an historic site simply on that basis. Free films shown at the Chamber of Commerce visitor center give a bit of history and a few directions around town, preparing you to tour some of the oldest homes and streets in the country.
Time: 8 a.m.-5:30 p.m.
Place: 10 Castillo Dr.
Contact: (904) 829-5681

Site of Slaughter

Fort Matanzas National Monument, which owes its name to the Spanish word for slaughter, marks the site where the Spaniard who founded St. Augustine killed more than 200 French citizens in 1565. The bloody act sealed Spain's domination of Florida for two centuries. The remains of the Spanish fort, on Rattlesnake

FLORIDA

St. Augustine

Island, are accessible by a free ferry.
Time: Mon., Wed., Fri., 9 a.m.-4:45 p.m.
Place: 14 mi. S of St. Augustine on FL A1A.
Contact: (904) 471-0116

St. Cloud

Glass Cutting

Learn about glass cutting at C. M. Bays Glassware, where a craftsman with 60 years' experience cuts glass tableware in his small shop. His trademarks are coasters cut with scenes of birds in courtship rituals.
Time: Mon.-Sat., 9:30 a.m.-5 p.m.
Place: 1213 Massachusetts Ave.
Contact: (305) 892-5533

Busy Cowboys

Call ahead and set up a tour of this ranch where you can watch cowboys at work. Desert Ranches, a 310,000-acre spread, is owned by the Mormon Church. The ranch has more than 50,000 head of cattle and many acres of citrus groves.
Time: Mon.-Fri., 7 a.m.-5 p.m.; tours by appt. only.
Place: 30 mi. E of town on FL 419.
Contact: (305) 892-3672

St. Petersburg

Planetarium and Observatory

Come and see a Friday evening planetarium show. If the sky is clear after the show, visitors have a chance to troop to the roof-top observatory at St. Petersburg Junior College to view the stars through a telescope.
Time: Planetarium: Fri., 7:30 p.m.
Place: Science Bldg., 6605 Fifth Ave. N.
Contact: (813) 381-0681

Free Fishing School

The St. Petersburg Rod and Gun Club offers newcomers

free fishing lessons. It is said, in fact, that the instructors can be proficient to the point of frustration: they can pull in fish after fish, while students stand next to them and try to imitate their techniques, but catch nothing. Fishing films are shown and equipment demonstrated.
Time: Jan.-Feb., Mon., 1 p.m.
Place: 3601 Ninth St.
Contact: (813) 898-0485

Free Newspapers

The publisher of the *St. Petersburg Evening Independent* is so sure of Florida's sunny weather he offers free papers to anyone on days there is absolutely no sun. The offer is good anywhere in the newspaper's circulation area.
Time: Dismal, dark days.
Place: Anywhere the paper is regularly sold.
Contact: (813) 893-8111

Museum of Fine Arts

One of the Museum of Fine Arts' most popular attractions is a small but good collection of Impressionist paintings. There also is Pre-Columbian gold and sculpture from India.
Time: Tues.-Sat., 10 a.m.-5 p.m.; Sun., 1-5 p.m. Tours: 2 p.m.
Place: 255 Beach Dr. N.
Contact: (813) 896-2667

Sanford

Golden Age Olympics

If you are over 55 and want to compete in athletic events that aren't too taxing, consider the Golden Age Olympics. The activities include a dance contest, a bicycle race, bowling matches and the unisex pancake race.
Time: 2nd week in Nov.
Place: Throughout the city.
Contact: (305) 322-2212

Sanibel

Beachcombing

Sanibel Island is a haven for beachcombers. In fact, a sort of hysteria sometimes seems to grip them and they are often seen thigh deep or deeper in the water, trying to uncover more shells. There is a bonus for beachcombers during the first weekend in March, when the Sanibel Shell Fair is in full swing.
Time: Anytime.
Place: Nearly anywhere on the island.
Contact: (813) 472-1080

Sarasota

Baroque Art

The John and Mable Ringling Museum of Art contains one of the most impressive collections of Baroque art on the continent, including several Rubens. The 68-acre grounds is beautifully landscaped.
Time: Free on Sat., 9 a.m.-5 p.m.
Place: 5401 Bayshore Dr.
Contact: (813) 355-5101
Note: The nearby Circus Museum and the Ringling home are not free on Sat.

Water-Ski Show

Water-skiing experts dazzle spectators with high-speed stunts—alone and in groups. You'll find these demonstrations at Island Park every spring.
Time: Early Feb.-Mar., Sun., 2 p.m.
Place: Marina on Hwy. 41.
Contact: (813) 955-8187

Spring Hill

Naked Chickens

A speed-plucking contest, Miss Drumstick pageant and zany stunts by a big cast of characters—take them all together and you have the Annual World Chicken-Plucking Contest. The highlight, of course, is the competition between four-person teams, each of which tries to pluck a dozen cluckers as quickly as possible.
Time: First week in Oct.
Place: Spring Hill Recreation Center.
Contact: (904) 796-2420

Tallahassee

Museum of Florida History

A mastodon skeleton, Spanish gold, a human skull and the curator's choice exhibit are among the displays at the Museum of Florida History. A feature that's perfect for children is "Grandmother Attic," where they can try on old dresses, shoes, hats and other clothes.
Time: Mon.-Sat., 9 a.m.-4:30 p.m.; Sun., 1-4:30 p.m.
Place: Pensacola and Bronough Sts.
Contact: (904) 488-1484

22-Story Capitol

The tours of this tall capitol include a sweeping view of Tallahassee from the top floor. The tour also includes a visit to House and Senate chambers.
Time: Mon.-Fri., 8:30 a.m.-4:30 p.m.; Sat.-Sun., 11 a.m.-4 p.m.
Place: S. Monroe St.
Contact: (904) 488-6167

Tampa

Brewery Tour

Free samples of beer—soft drinks for non-drinkers—are offered before and after tours

FLORIDA

Tampa

of the Joseph Schlitz Brewery. Tours begin every 30 minutes.
Time: Mon.-Fri., 10 a.m.-3 p.m.
Place: 11111 N. 30th St.
Contact: (813) 971-7070

Canoe Trip

The Alafia River, after running 25 miles through wooded Florida countryside, spills into Tampa Bay. The picturesque stream is sometimes still, sometimes quickly flowing, though there are no major rapids. Another good canoe trip is along the Manatee River from the Manatee River Road to Bradenton. Call the contact below for more details.
Time: Anytime.
Contact: (813) 228-7777

Cigar Making

Tour the Villazon Cigar factory to see how cigars are made—both by machine and by hand. The best, of course, are always wrapped, bound and rolled by skilled workers. The tours last a half-hour.
Time: Mon.-Thurs., 9:30 a.m. and 2:30 p.m.
Place: 3104 N. Armenia Ave.
Contact: (813) 879-2291

Free Bees

Tampa's five "Free Bees"— buses disguised as cable cars—run the downtown streets and are free to anyone who hops aboard. The vehicles stop along the pedestrian mall, at major offices and stores, and at parking areas surrounding downtown.
Time: Mon.-Fri., 6:45 a.m.-6:45 p.m.
Place: Downtown.
Contact: (813) 251-1078

Moorish Building

The old Tampa Bay Hotel, now owned by the University of Tampa, was built in 1891 to look like the Moorish Alhambra. Its original cost was almost $3.5 million. Home for Teddy Roosevelt and the Rough Riders during the Spanish-American War, its historical interest adds to its architectural charm.
Time: Tours: Sept.-May, Tues.-Thurs., 1:30 p.m.
Place: 401 W. Kennedy Blvd.
Contact: (813) 253-8861, ext. 441

Planetarium Show

The University of South Florida puts on free planetarium shows. The presentations last for an hour and are changed every two months. Some recent shows featured a presentation on the Christmas Star and a description of navigating by the stars.
Time: Oct.-mid-June, Sun., p.m.
Place: Fowler Ave. on University of South Florida campus.
Contact: (813) 974-3010
Note: Be sure to make a reservation in advance.

Pirates

Every year a crew of pirates sails into Tampa harbor in a fully rigged ship and invades

the city. Once their attack is launched, they lead floats and bands on a three-hour parade through town. Then there is the feast: free Spanish bean soup and Cuban bread.
Time: First Mon. after first Tues. in Feb.
Place: Tampa waterfront.
Contact: (813) 228-7777

Ybor City

Ybor City is Tampa's Latin section, founded by Cubans who left their native country in the 1800s. What was once a cluster of cigar factories has been turned into small shops and restaurants. Red-tile roofs, wrought-iron balconies and fountains add flavor to this part of town.
Time: Anytime.
Place: Eastern section of town.
Contact: (813) 228-7777

Tarpon Springs

Greek Cross Ceremony

After the Epiphany Mass at St. Nicholas Greek Orthodox Church, there is the diving for the cross. A small cross is carried through town during a parade and then thrown into a bayou, where boys dive for it. The one who brings it to the surface gets a trophy.
Time: Jan. 6, noon.
Place: N. Pinellas Ave.
Contact: (813) 937-3540

Sponge Auction

Giant sponges that divers haul up from the deep are sold at the Sponge Dock and Market, but there's more to the area than that. There are shrimp boats, gift shops, a Greek church, artists and all the hustle and bustle you'd expect at a port.
Time: Schedule of activity varies.
Place: On Dodecanese Blvd.
Contact: (813) 937-6109

Titusville

Canaveral National Seashore

More than 280 varieties of birds have been seen in the Canaveral National Seashore or the nearby Merritt Island National Wildlife Refuge. But birdwatching isn't the only free activity at the seashore. Visitors can swim, picnic or comb the beaches for shells and other items.
Time: Dawn to dusk.
Place: 7 mi. E of town on FL 402.
Contact: (305) 867-4675

Vero Beach

Boater's Outing

The pelican, known for its spectacular plunges into schools of fish at feeding time, is one of Florida's great attractions. Pelican Island on the Indian River is a haven for these large birds. More than 3,500 pelicans hatch there each year. The island is easily accessible by boat—a terrific day's outing.
Time: Anytime.
Place: 15 mi. N. of Vero Beach.
Contact: (305) 567-3491

West Palm Beach

Chinese Art

The Norton Gallery and School of Art boasts one of the finest collections of Chinese art in the Southeast. The sculpture and other works of jade, bronze and ceramics go back to the seventh century. Other major exhibits include French paintings and sculpture of the late 19th and early 20th centuries and modern American works.
Time: Gallery: Tues.-Fri., 10 a.m.-5 p.m.; Sat.-Sun., 1-5 p.m. Guided tours: Sun., 2 p.m.
Place: 1451 S. Olive Ave.
Contact: (305) 832-5194

Winter Park

Botanical Garden

There are five greenhouses filled with orchids at this natural 55-acre setting, which includes a small pond. There also is a picnic pavillion.
Time: 8 a.m.-dusk.
Place: Denning and Garden Drs.
Contact: (305) 644-9860

FLORIDA

Statewide

Beach Drive

A hundred miles of road stretch along the sparkling, nearly snow-white beaches of the Florida panhandle. Much of the time, motorists can drive along for miles, their view of the ocean unobstructed. Call or write the contact below for a brochure on the beach area; ask for the "Vacation Package."
Contact: Department of Commerce, Division of Tourism, 126 Van Buren St., Tallahassee, FL 32301; (904) 487-1462

Salt-water Fishing

Florida is especially well-known to sportsmen for its good fishing for a variety of salt-water species. You'll find good spots along nearly any coastline, in the keys and in many brackish rivers. And it's free. No licenses are needed.
Time: Anytime.
Contact: Florida Dept. of Natural Resources, 3900 Commonwealth Blvd., Tallahassee, FL 32303; (904) 488-7326.

Pro Baseball Training Camps

Pitchers, batters, fielders, catchers—you'll find professional baseball players in their training camps during the spring months throughout

Florida. Stop in to watch your favorite pros train and rookies try out for the coming season at any one of the fields listed below. A perfect outing for anyone who loves this all-American sport.
Team: Pittsburgh Pirates
Time: Feb. 26-Mar. 12, 10 a.m.-1 p.m.
Place: Pirate City, Bradenton.
Contact: (813) 747-3031
Team: Philadelphia Phillies
Time: Feb. 26-Mar. 12, 10 a.m.-1 p.m.
Place: Carpentar Field Complex, Clearwater.
Contact: (813) 443-0602
Team: Houston Astros
Time: Feb. 20-Mar. 12, 10 a.m.-1 p.m.
Place: Cocoa Stadium, Cocoa.
Contact: (305) 632-5200
Team: New York Yankees
Time: Feb. 19-Mar. 10, 10 a.m.-1 p.m.
Place: Ft. Lauderdale Stadium, 5301 NW 12th Ave., Ft. Lauderdale.
Contact: (305) 776-1921
Team: Kansas City Royals
Time: Feb. 22-Mar. 10, 10 a.m.-1 p.m.
Place: Terry Park, Ft. Meyers.
Contact: (813) 337-1624
Team: Baltimore Orioles
Time: Feb. 25-Mar. 11, 10 a.m.-1 p.m.
Place: Miami Stadium, 2301 NW Tenth Ave., Miami.
Contact: (305) 635-5395

Team: Minnesota Twins
Time: Feb. 22-Mar. 7, 10 a.m.-1 p.m.
Place: Tinker Field, Orlando.
Contact: (305) 849-6346
Team: Texas Rangers
Time: Feb. 24-Mar. 9, 10 a.m.-1 p.m.
Place: Municipal Stadium, 1601 NE Eighth St., Pompano Beach.
Contact: (305) 943-4873
Team: Chicago White Sox
Time: Feb. 24-Mar. 11, 10 a.m.-1 p.m.
Place: 12th St. and Tuttle Ave., Sarasota.
Contact: (813) 366-1745
Team: Cincinnati Reds
Time: Feb. 25-Mar. 12, 10 a.m.-1 p.m.
Place: Redsland, Tampa.
Contact: (813) 877-9340
Team: Los Angeles Dodgers
Time: Feb. 26-Mar. 10, 10 a.m.-1 p.m.
Place: Holman Field, Vero Beach.
Contact: (305) 569-4900
Team: Montreal Expos
Time: Feb. 25-Mar. 9, 10 a.m.-2 p.m.
Place: Municipal Stadium, West Palm Beach.
Contact: (305) 684-6801
Team: Boston Red Sox
Time: Feb. 24-Mar. 9, 10 a.m.-1 p.m.
Place: Chain O'Lakes Park, Winter Haven.
Contact: (813) 293-3900

GEORGIA

⭐ **ATLANTA**

• **Macon**

• **Columbus**

Savannah •

GEORGIA

Andersonville

Confederate Military Prison

Much of the exterior of the village of Andersonville has been restored, making it worth a look in itself. Nearby is the Andersonville National Historic Site with a national cemetery and a 26-acre stockade, where up to 32,000 soldiers were kept in the Civil War's most infamous prison. There's a small museum and daily slide shows.
Time: May 15-Aug., 8:30 a.m.-7 p.m.; Sept.-May 14, 8:30 a.m.-5 p.m.
Place: On GA 49, 9 mi. NE of Americus, in E Andersonville.
Contact: (912) 924-0343

Athens

American Paintings

In the Georgia Museum of Art you'll find a dozen study pieces from the Kress Collection and a solid core of American paintings, most of which date from the early part of the 20th century. Altogether, the museum has 5,000 works of art, including those on paper.
Time: Sept.-May, Mon.-Fri., 9 a.m.-5 p.m.; Sat., 9 a.m.-noon; Sun., 2-5 p.m.
Place: On the University of Georgia campus, Jackson St. N.
Contact: (404) 542-3254

Historic Walking-Driving Tours

A brochure outlines four walking-driving tours of one of Georgia's most interesting towns. It is noted for its well-preserved antebellum houses. You can walk the historic downtown area and the campus of the University of Georgia. It's best to drive along Prince and Milledge Avenues. Write ahead for a free brochure.
Time: Mon.-Sat., 9 a.m.-5 p.m.; Sun., 2-5 p.m.
Place: 280 E. Dougherty St.
Contact: Athens Convention and Visitors Bureau, P.O. Box 948, Athens, GA 30603; (404) 549-6800.

Oldest Remaining Residence

The restored Church-Waddel-Brumby House (named, in part, for two former presidents of the University of Georgia who owned the house) dates back to 1820. There are many unusual pieces of period furniture in this house, which now serves as the town's Welcome Center. You can pick up numerous free brochures about the surrounding area while you're at the Center.
Time: Mon.-Sat., 9 a.m.-5 p.m.; Sun., 2-5 p.m.
Place: 280 E. Dougherty St.
Contact: (404) 546-1805

Star Gazing

The local astronomy club meets twice a month or so to look through the University's telescopes at whatever is the most interesting at the time. If you'd like to join the group, call ahead for dates and details.
Place: Astronomy Dept. on the University of Georgia campus.
Contact: University of Georgia, Athens, GA 30602; (404) 542-2485, ext. 44.

A Tree That Owns Itself

This tree grows on land deeded to it by its predecessor, which was blown over in 1942. The sapling planted in 1946 has since grown to considerable size, but it's still not large enough to take up the 25 square feet it owns according to its title deed!
Place: Dearing and Finley Sts.

World's Largest Framed Oil Painting

This painting depicts the interior of St. Peter's Cathedral

and dominates the interior of the Greek Revival chapel. It weighs over a ton and is 17 by 23-1/2 feet in size. The painting was completed in 1847.
Place: Chapel on University of Georgia campus.
Contact: (404) 542-3354

World's Only Double-Barreled Cannon

This unusual cannon with two barrels was cast in the Athens Foundry in 1863 during the Civil War. It was meant to fire two cannonballs simultaneously with the balls being linked by a chain. Lack of synchronization nearly killed the men firing the cannon, which instantly became a relic.
Place: City Hall lawn, College and Hancock Aves.
Contact: (404) 549-6800

Atlanta

Contemporary Art

Although the High Museum of Art has pieces from many periods, including a small part of the Kress collection, it features contemporary art. There are also changing exhibits and a good collection of porcelains.
Time: Tues.-Sat., 10 a.m.-5 p.m.; Sun., noon-5 p.m.
Place: 1280 Peachtree St. NE, at 15th St.
Contact: (404) 892-3600

Dr. Martin L. King Jr. Memorial

Here you can visit the grave of the noted civil rights leader who received the Nobel Peace Prize in 1964.
Place: 413 Auburn Ave.

Dogwood Festival

The city of Atlanta looks like it has been covered with new-fallen snow at the height of the dogwood season, celebrated throughtout Georgia in early April. Altanta has had a Dogwood Festival since 1936, but it has only been extremely popular in the last decade, drawing up to a half million people in recent years. For a list of all the events, write to the contact below.
Time: 2nd full week in April.
Contact: Atlanta Dogwood Festival, 33 North Ave., Suite 540, Atlanta, GA 30308; (404) 892-0539.

Fernbank Museum

This is a small, but quite good exhibit hall of natural history and space science. There's a dinosaur exhibit, mounted animals (including a bear), the Apollo 6 capsule, and a Mars display.
Time: Mon., 8:30 a.m.-5 p.m.; Tues.-Fri., 8:30 a.m.-10 p.m.; Sat., 8:30 a.m.-5 p.m.; Sun., 1:30-5 p.m.
Place: 156 Heaton Park Dr.
Contact: (404) 378-4311

Governor's Mansion

You're invited to tour the Governor's Mansion. Tours cover the eight rooms on the first floor and the grounds. You'll find hostesses in each room to answer questions and give background information. The Greek Revival-style building was built in 1968 and is well worth a visit.
Time: Tues.-Thurs., 10-11:45 a.m.
Place: 391 W. Paces Ferry Rd.
Contact: (404) 261-1776

GEORGIA

Atlanta

Margaret Mitchell's Grave

This is one of the more interesting and beautiful cemeteries in the Southeast. It's noted for its Victorian statuary and for being the final resting place of some famous people, including author Margaret Mitchell and golfer Bobby Jones.
Time: Sunrise to sunset.
Place: 248 Oakland Ave.
Contact: (404) 577-8163

Palatial Homes

The northwest section of Atlanta has some of the Southeast's most palatial homes. They are at their very best in the second and third weeks of April, with the dogwoods and azaleas in full bloom. Highly recommended are drives along Habersham Road, Peach Tree Battle Avenue, and West Paces Ferry Road.

River Rafting

While there's a charge to join the Great Rambling River Raft Race on the Chattahoochee River on the third Saturday in May, the rest of the year you can bob down the river on an inner tube without being elbow to elbow to 250,000 rafters. And for free! The water temperature is warmest from August to early October. The best stretch of river runs from Morgan Falls to the section that flows under Highway 41.

Largest Southeast Farmers Market

Twenty thousand people shop for fresh produce in this 146-acre market on the outskirts of the city each day. It is one of the most impressive and colorful in the country, with special festivals in June and August, the latter including country music bands. A happening!
Time: 24 hrs. a day.
Place: 10 mi. S of Atlanta off I-75; 16 Forest Parkway.
Contact: (404) 366-6910

A 27-pound Gold Bar

At the Monetary Museum in the Federal Reserve Bank you can see 29 panels giving information on transactions from ancient bartering to present-day trading with paper bills. On display is a 27-pound gold bar and uncut sheets of varying values of money—up to $100,000 bills.
Time: Mon.-Fri., 11 a.m.-2 p.m. By appt. only!
Place: 104 Marietta St.
Contact: (404) 586-8500

Augusta

Lovely Romanesque Church

This very large Romanesque church was built in 1898 with 15 patterns of brick, making it quite ornate. Its stained glass windows were imported from Munich.
Time: 9 a.m.-5 p.m.
Place: Sacred Heart Catholic Church, Greene and 13th Sts.
Contact: (404) 724-2324

An Historic Church

Augusta was founded in this spot in 1735. The church was built 15 years later and is one of the most impressive in the state, partly because of its size and partly because of its lovely stained glass windows. Take a look too at the cemetery.
Time: Mon.-Fri., 9 a.m.-5 p.m.; Sat., 9 a.m.-noon. Sunday services, 8:30 a.m., 11 a.m.
Place: S bank of Savannah R., at 605 Reynolds.
Contact: (404) 724-2485

One of Augusta's Oldest Homes

Once thought to be the oldest home in Augusta, the Harris Pearson Walker House is now believed to date from 1797—still old indeed. It has been restored and contains many pieces from the early 1800s.

Time: By appt. only.
Place: 1822 Broad St.
Contact: (404) 724-2324

A Cursed Column

The Old Slave Market Column was cursed by a preacher who was forbidden to preach in this section of town. So look but don't touch—the curse is said to affect all who do. Unless you're interested in red light districts, you'll want to see the column during the day.

Place: Broad and Fifth Sts.

Ware's Folly

One of the more beautiful historic homes in Augusta. It was built in 1818 for $40,000, a cost thought at that time to be exorbitant. Inside you'll find a small art gallery.

Time: Tues.-Fri., 10 a.m.-4 p.m. (closed for lunch); Sat., 4-6 p.m.
Place: 506 Telfair St.
Contact: (404) 722-5495

Brunswick

Blessing of the Shrimp Fleet

Brunswick calls itself the capital of the shrimp world. And here, as along the entire coast, you can witness the blessing of the fleet, with its attendant games, carnival atmosphere and colorfully decorated shrimp boats.

Time: Mother's Day weekend. Festivities begin Fri. with the blessing on Sun. morning.
Place: Docks on Bay St.
Contact: (912) 265-0620

Chatsworth

Carter's Lake

A dam has formed an enormous lake in this section of northwestern Georgia. Not only do the overlooks afford lovely views of the surrounding foothills of the Blue Ridge Mountains, but trails lead to hidden and remote areas of great scenic charm. A fine area for hiking.

Place: 9 mi. SE of town.

Claxton

World's Largest Fruitcake Bakery

From August to mid-December this bakery churns out 100,000 pounds of fruitcake every day! That adds up to millions of pounds per year. You'll see everything from mixing to

boxing on this once-in-a-lifetime tour, which ends with a sample, of course.

Time: Mon.-Sat., 8 a.m.-6 p.m.
Place: In front of water tower on US 301, GA 280.
Contact: (912) 739-3441

Clayton

White Water

Looking for a challenge? You'll find 30 rapids here with Class III or greater difficulty on a six-mile stretch of Georgia's most turbulent river, the Chattooga.

Contact: (404) 536-0081 or 878-2541

GEORGIA

Columbus

US Army Infantry Museum

This is one of the largest exhibits of weapons and warfare history in the country, with separate displays for each of the wars and a Medal of Honor Section.

Time: Tues.-Fri., 10 a.m.-4:30 p.m.; Sat.-Sun., 12:30-4:30 p.m.
Place: At Ft. Benning, on Ingersol St.
Contact: (404) 545-2958

Handmade Peanut Butter Logs

On a tour of Tom's Foods you'll see how peanut butter logs are made from scratch. You'll also see shelling, cooking and packaging machines for potloads of peanuts. At the end of the tour you're encouraged to nibble on two free packs of peanuts and a pair of candy bars.

Time: June-Aug., Mon.-Fri., 9:30 and 10:30 a.m.; Sept.-May, Tues.-Wed., 9:30 and 10:30 a.m. By appt. only.
Place: 900 Eighth St. at Tenth Ave.
Contact: Alex Conniff, (404) 323-2721, ext. 197.

Parachute Drops

Take in the Airborne show at one of the nation's largest military posts. But be sure to check into exact dates and times, or you'll end up seeing only training!

Time: Airborne shows: Usually Mon. a.m.
Place: Eubanks Field at Ft. Benning.
Contact: Public Affairs Office, Community Relations, Infantry Center, Ft. Benning, GA 31905; (404) 545-3512.

Conyers

Visit a Monastery

There are only ten monasteries in the country. This one is similar in style to a 12th-century structure, with 2,000 acres of grounds, greenhouses and a gift shop. There's even a lake with a picnic area.

Time: Mon.-Sat., 10-11:30 a.m.
Place: 8 mi. SW of town via GA 138, GA 212.
Contact: (404) 483-8705

Cuthbert

Southern Homes

Take a tour of Cuthbert to get a glimpse of fine Southern homes. You'll find equally classic mansions in Athens,

Augusta, Madison and Washington.

Time: Mon.-Fri., 9 a.m.-5 p.m.
Place: Chamber of Commerce, Town Square.
Contact: (912) 732-2683

Dahlonega

Gold Panning

Pan for gold in some of the streams around Dahlonega, the site of the first gold rush in 1828. During Gold Rush Days on the third weekend in October, you'll hear hog calling, local bands and laughter in an open carnival that's free of charge to everyone.

Contact: (404) 864-3711

729-Foot Falls

The Amicalola Falls are the highest in the state, and you can get drenched by the spray at their base. There's also a bridge which crosses them at the top of the cliff. An 8.7-mile trail leads to Springer Mountain, the start of the Appalachian Trail which extends for 2,000 miles to Maine. The area is noted for brilliant colors in spring when the rhododendrons bloom and for its fall foliage in October.

Place: 18 mi. S of town via GA 19, 52.
Contact: (404) 265-2885

Folkston

Okefenokee Swamp

You have access to this famous swamp through the Suwanee Canal Recreation Area. Here you'll find a 4,000-foot boardwalk, which leads to an observation tower. During the off-season you can drive your car to the boardwalk. In the summer, however, there's a small charge for a tram which takes you there. Note that the off-season is not the best time to see the animals in this area, but you can see a wide variety of plants and a few cold-weather animals.

Time: Mar.-mid-Sept., 7 a.m.-7:30 p.m.; mid-Sept.-Feb., 8 a.m.-6 p.m.
Place: 11 mi. SW of Folkston via GA 23, 121.
Contact: (912) 496-7836

Fort Oglethorpe

Markers and Monuments

Hundreds of markers, monuments and placards at the Chickamauga-Chattanooga National Military Park help you understand this huge battle area on a combined walking and driving tour. Thousands of troops died here daily during the Civil War. A museum in the park has a 355-piece collection of military weapons.

Time: Mon.-Sun., 8 a.m.-4:45 p.m.
Place: 3 mi. S of town on US 27.
Contact: (404) 866-9241

Fort Valley

Seven Acres Of Camellias

The American Camellia Society tends a greenhouse and seven acres of camellias which burst into bloom from November to March, with peak color usually in late January and early February. The society also has an extensive gallery of Boehm porcelain sculptures.

Time: Gardens: always open. Gallery: Mon.-Fri., 9 a.m.-4 p.m. (closed during lunch).
Place: 5 mi. SW of town via GA 49.
Contact: (912) 967-2358

Peach Blossom Tour

Fort Valley is known as the "peach capital" of Georgia, with thousands of fruit trees in full blossom in mid-March. An ideal drive would take you along US 341. The fruit is ripe from June through August.

Hartwell

Hartwell Lake Reservoir

Free tours take place daily at the Resource Manager's Office at the Hartwell Dam, which holds back 56,000 acres of water in its reservoir. It's very popular with largemouth bass fishermen, boaters and campers (only a few free primitive campsites, others with admission). You can find freshwater shellfish that are edible; some even produce pearls—free if you find one!

Time: Tours: Mon. and Fri., 2:30 p.m.; Sat.-Sun., 1:30 p.m. and 3 p.m.
Place: 6 mi. N of town via US 29.
Contact: (404) 376-4788

Helen

An Alpine Village

Touristy, yes, but an Alpine village in a scenic setting. Don't miss the Old Sautee Store and Anna Ruby Falls 1-1/2 miles north of Unicoi State Park.

Hiawassee

Lovely Scenic Drive

Northeastern Georgia is one of the most beautiful sections of the state, with its mountain

Hiawassee

scenery and spectacular drives. One of the best scenic drives runs along US 76 from Hiawassee to Blairsville. Get your camera out just before you dip into the village of Young Harris. You can then drive south of Blairsville via US 19/129, then east via GA 180 and north on GA 66 to Brasstown Bald, the highest peak in Georgia. This peak has an observation tower that also offers a film on the changing of the seasons.

Contact: US Forestry Service, 601 Broad St., Gainesville, GA 30501; (404) 536-0541.

Semi-Precious Stones

Rockhounders take note: the area around Hiawassee is noted for its many minerals including amethyst crystal, one of the most valuable semiprecious stones. Inquire locally for hints to aid your search.

Jekyll Island

Shelling

Looking for shells along the coast is one activity which appeals to many of the state's visitors. You'll find good shelling on Jekyll, St. Simons, Sapelo, and Cumberland Islands. Note that both Jekyll and St. Simons are accessible by car.

Macon

Indian Ceremonial Mounds

At the Ocmulgee National Monument you can learn about the six different cultures that lived in this area over a period of 10,000 years. You can also enter a large ceremonial earth lodge and watch Creek, Seminole and Cherokee Indians demonstrating craft skills in the summer. A recently completed 20-minute film is available for viewing.

Time: June-Aug., 9 a.m.-7 p.m.; Sept.-May, 9 a.m.-5 p.m.
Place: E Macon on US 80, at 1207 Emery Hwy.
Contact: (912) 742-0447

Marietta

Site of Major Civil War Battle

The Kinnesaw Mountain National Battlefield Park is of historic interest with only the earthworks preserved. A visitor center has both slide shows and exhibits.

Time: Park: May-Aug., 8:30 a.m.-7 p.m.; Sept.-Apr., 8:30 a.m.-6 p.m. Visitor center: May-Aug., 8:30 a.m.-6 p.m.; Sept.-Apr., 8:30 a.m.-5 p.m.
Place: 2 mi. N of town off US 41.
Contact: (404) 427-4686

Milledgeville

Flannery O'Connor Collections

Take a tour through this lovely town noted for its antebellum homes and stop off at the library on the campus of Georgia College to see the Flannery O'Connor Collections of memorabilia and manuscripts, if you're interested in her life and work.

Time: Library: Mon.-Fri., 8 a.m.-5 p.m.
Place: Campus of Georgia College.
Contact: (912) 453-5573
Note: Research by prior arrangement only.

Perry

A Free Ferry Ride

Follow GA 127 west from Perry and you'll cross the Flint River on the last ferry boat in Georgia. The 15-minute ride is free. Note that this route takes you

past the camellia gardens (see Fort Valley-Marshallville).

Place: 4 mi. SW of town on GA 40.

Note: Honk horn for service anytime during daylight.

Free Beer

End an extensive tour of the Pabst Brewing Company with two free beers in the hospitality room (soft drinks for the kids).

Time: Tours: Mon.-Fri., 9-11 a.m. and 1-4 p.m., on the hour.

Place: 7 mi. S of Perry via US 341, GA Spur 247.

Contact: (912) 987-3639

Rome

Georgia's Best-Kept Secret

Don't miss the Martha Berry Museum and Oak Hill Plantation. The plantation, dating back to 1847, is filled with priceless antiques and is a fine example of antebellum architecture. The museum houses a collection of European art. The gardens are being reshaped to represent a bygone era.

Time: Tues.-Sat., 10 a.m.-5 p.m.; Sun., 1-5 p.m.

Place: 2 mi. N of town via US 27.

Contact: (404) 291-1883

Note: The last 2 weeks in Apr. and the 1st week in May is the ideal time to see the dogwood!

St. Simon's Island

Britain's Largest American Fort

Fort Frederica National Monument consists of the excavated foundations of Great Britain's largest fort in America. There's a visitor center with a 25-minute film on the lives and times of the fort's inhabitants.

Time: June-Aug., 8 a.m.-6 p.m.; Sept.-May, 8 a.m.-5 p.m. Movie on the hour from 9 a.m.-4 p.m.

Place: NW end of island on Frederica Rd.

Contact: (912) 638-3639

Savannah

Great Historic Tour

This is one of the great walking tours of the US, which will take you through historic streets to 1,100 architecturally significant buildings, 19 parklike squares, and a waterfront that's too beautiful to believe. Begin the tour at the Savannah Visitors Center where you can see a free slide presentation and pick up a walking tour brochure (also free). Note that the center was once a railroad station built in 1860.

Time: Center: Mon.-Fri., 8:30 a.m.-5 p.m.; Sat.-Sun., 9 a.m.-5 p.m.

Place: 301 W. Broad St.

Contact: (912) 233-6651

Note: Savannah is heaven during the last 2 weeks of April when the flowers are in full bloom!

40,000 Cookies an Hour

Byrde Cookie Shanty really cooks those cookies, 40,000 an hour to be precise. Take a 20-minute tour to see how these delicious wafers are produced and taste a few in the bargain!

Time: Mon.-Fri., 9 a.m.-4 p.m.

Place: 2233 Norwood Ave.

Contact: (912) 355-1716

Suwanee

Falcons' Football Practice

In late summer you can watch the Atlanta Falcons practice football here in training sessions two times a day free of charge. Be sure to call ahead for exact hours of training.
Time: Twice daily, mid-July-Aug.
Place: Suwanee, 30 mi. N of Atlanta on I-85N, exit 44.
Contact: (404) 588-1111

Thomasville

Rose City

This town is noted for its roses. You'll find test gardens for these lovely flowers east of town. The 2,000 rose bushes burst into bloom from mid-April to October. They're usually at their peak during the Rose Fest in the fourth week of April.
Time: Mon.-Sat., 8 a.m.-5 p.m.; Sun., 2-5 p.m.
Place: 2 mi. E on US 84.
Contact: (912) 226-5568

Toomsboro

Amateur Musician Launching Pad

At the Swampland Opera House you can hear amateur musicians try to launch careers in country, western, bluegrass and gospel music—at no charge.
Time: Fri., 7-11 p.m.; Sat., 4 p.m.-midnight.
Place: 6 mi. E of US 441 via GA 57.
Contact: (912) 933-5713

Washington

Antebellum Homes Driving Tour

Pick up a brochure with a free map of 75 historic Washington landmarks at the contact listed below. You can take a driving tour along the suggested route and see many antebellum homes, historical markers, churches and lovely scenery. Although you cannot enter the historic homes, the tour is a beautiful introduction to the architecture of the area.
Time: Chamber of Commerce: Mon., Tues., Thurs. and Fri., 8:30 a.m.-4:30 p.m.; Wed., 8:30 a.m.-noon.
Contact: Wilkes County Chamber of Commerce, 25 E Square (Town Square); (404) 678-2013.

LOUISIANA

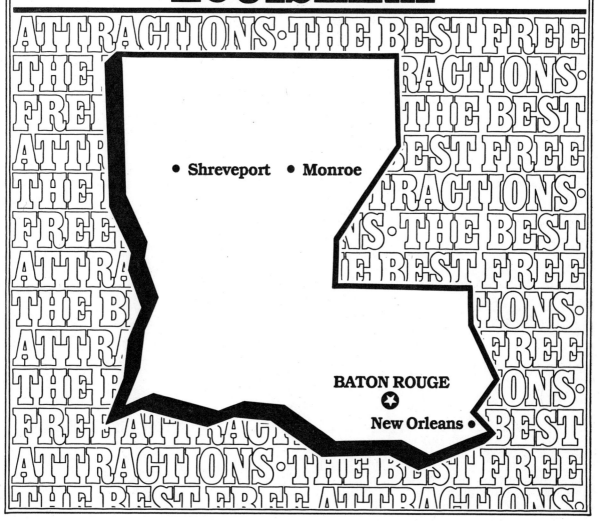

- Shreveport - Monroe

BATON ROUGE
★
New Orleans •

LOUISIANA

Alexandria

Kisatchie National Forest

Take a walk along the state's largest hiking trail. You're liable to stumble onto pieces of petrified palm, discover free camping areas, or picnic among dogwood and wild azalea. Louisiana's only national forest covers 595,000 acres and includes facilities for fishing, swimming, water-skiing, boating and hunting.

Place: N, W and S of town.
Contact: Kisatchie National Forest, 2500 Shreveport Highway, Pineville, LA 71360; (318) 445-6511, ext. 301.
Note: Fees may be charged at recreation sites. Inquire for details.

Baton Rouge

Arts and Science Center

Housed in a magnificent 56-year-old railway station, the Louisiana Arts and Science Center and Riverside Museum contain fine arts exhibits, an authentic mummy and historical and scientific displays. Among the featured attractions are an exhibit of vintage train cars and a three-dimensional display illustrating Mississippi River channel changes.

Time: Tues.-Sat., 10 a.m.-5 p.m.; Sun., 1 a.m.-5 p.m.
Place: 502 North Blvd.
Contact: P.O. Box 3373, Baton Rouge, LA 70821; (504) 344-9463.
Note: Museum is open free of charge every Tues. Arts and Science Center is free everyday.

America's Tallest State Capitol

The tallest state capitol in America rises 34 floors above formal gardens to an observation deck offering a scenic view of the Mississippi River and the city. Made of 30 kinds of construction marble from around the world, the magnificent structure features an impressive array of murals, a sunken garden and an old arsenal museum with ancient costumes and historic maps. It also contains the spot where Governor Huey Long was assassinated in 1935.

Time: 8 a.m.-4 p.m. Tours every hour on the hour.
Place: N. Third St. and Boyd Ave.
Contact: (504) 342-7317

Old State Capitol

Erected in 1847, the Old State Capitol served as the home of Louisiana State government until 1932. It resembles an historic Gothic Revival castle and sits atop a lush green hillside overlooking the Mississippi River. Among its most interesting features is a massive spiral stairway that winds upward toward a stained glass dome. It also contains a war museum and contemporary art exhibits.

Time: Mon.-Fri., 9:30 a.m.-5 p.m.; Sat. and holidays, 10 a.m.-5 p.m. Sun., 1-5 p.m.
Place: North Blvd. and Phillips St.
Contact: (504) 383-1825

Old Pentagon

These four brick buildings, built in 1822, served as Army barracks for many years and as dormitories for Louisiana State University from 1886 to 1925. Many famous military figures visited or resided here—Lafayette; President Zachary Taylor; Generals Lee, Grant, Sheridan and Custer; and Jefferson Davis.

Place: Corner of River Rd. and State Capitol Ave.
Contact: (504) 343-6379

Rural Life Museum

Life on a 19th-century Louisiana plantation is depicted at the Burden Research Plantation, which contains a commissary, sugar mill, church and smithy. A large warehouse

houses wagons, carriages, plantation bells and vintage farm equipment.
Time: Mon.-Fri., 8:30 a.m.-noon; 1-4 p.m., by appt. only.
Place: 4560 Essen Ln. at I-10.
Contact: (504) 766-8241
Note: Children not admitted.

Louisiana State University

Established in 1860 near Alexandria, Louisiana State University was moved to Baton Rouge in 1869 and now enrolls about 26,600 students. Among the sites to see on campus are Memorial Tower, an outdoor Greek Theater, and Natural Science and Rural Life Museums.
Time: Tours of campus: Mon.-Fri., 8 a.m.-4:30 p.m.; Sat., 9 a.m.-noon and 1-4:30 p.m.; Sun., 1-4:30 p.m.
Place: Highland Rd. on the SW edge of town.
Contact: (504) 388-8451
Note: Ask contact for hours of specific sites and special events.

Wild Animals in the Woods

More than 500 animals from six continents roam the natural settings in this 140-acre wooded area. You can see these animals by hiking across a walkway overlooking enclosed

habitats or by taking a sidewalk tram or miniature train.
Time: Free on Sat., 9 a.m.-noon.
Place: On Thomas Rd., 1 mi. E of LA 19.
Contact: (504) 775-3877

Bozier

Scenic Drive

One of the most scenic routes in Louisiana is the 18-mile Dogwood Trail Drive. This trail passes near Bozier and is a stunning stretch of flowers when the dogwood is in bloom, usually for a month following Easter. Call the contact listed below for information about the exact route of the trail; the route may vary from year to year.
Time: Mon.-Fri., 8:30 a.m.-5 p.m.
Contact: (318) 746-0252

Breaux Bridge

Crawfish Racing and Eating Contest

The entire community of Breaux Bridge and an estimated 100,000 visitors turn out every year for this unique event on the banks of the Bayou Teche. This biennial tribute to a lowly crustacean features a festival parade, crawfish race, and crawfish peeling and eating contest. Word has it that the record

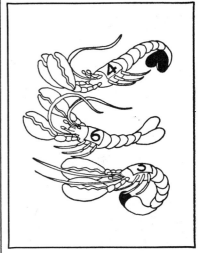

crawfish consumption for the event is 33 pounds.
Time: One weekend each May of even-numbered years.
Contact: (318) 332-2172

Buras

Fort Jackson

Built in 1822-32 to protect the river approach to New Orleans, this massive masonry fort was occupied by Confederate troops early in the Civil War and sustained a week of shelling by Union gunboats. It contains picnic grounds, mysterious old corridors and a museum.
Time: 10 a.m.-sunset.
Place: S of town on LA 23.
Contact: (504) 527-6900

LOUISIANA

Cameron

Wildlife Industries Celebration

Rock jetties extend into the Gulf waters right along Main Street here, providing casting spots for fishermen and tie-ups for colorful shrimp boats. The town hosts the Louisiana Fur and Wildlife Festival each winter in honor of the local industries. There are competitions in duck calling, trap setting, muskrat skinning, oyster shucking, shrimp heading, archery, trap shooting, field dog trialing and so on. A parade, beauty pageant and crafts booths round out the festival.

Time: Festival: early Jan.
Contact: (318) 775-5551

Carville

Leprosy Hospital

This US Public Health Service Hospital is the only medical facility in the continental US devoted to the research and treatment of leprosy. The modern treatment of the disease was discovered here. Walking tours of the scenic grounds are conducted daily. See also the old plantation mansion called Indian Camp.

Place: On LA 141, 4 mi. W of LA 75.
Contact: (504) 642-7771

Chalmette

Chalmette National Historical Park

Site of Andrew Jackson's famous Battle of New Orleans in 1815, which ended the War of 1812 and paved the way for westward expansion and made Jackson a national hero. A one-mile tour of the historic battlefield is offered along with exhibits and audio-visual demonstrations in the visitor center, located in a restored antebellum home.

Time: 8 a.m.-5 p.m.; closed Mardi Gras.
Place: 6 mi. NE of town on St. Bernard Hwy. (LA 46).
Contact: (504) 271-2412

Fisher

Preserved Sawmill Town

Historic preservation buffs will marvel at the way the original structures of this turn-of-the-century sawmill town have been retained. The homes, picket fences, commissary, opera house and depot look much as they did when Fisher was founded in 1897.

Place: On US 171.

Fort Polk

Fort Polk Military Museum

This museum, built in 1941, features vivid displays of flags, uniforms, military equipment and vehicles dating from the Revolution to the present.

Time: Mon.-Fri., 8 a.m.-4 p.m.; Sat.-Sun., 8 a.m.-5 p.m.
Place: On LA 467, just N of LA 10.
Contact: (318) 537-7905

Galliano

Oyster Eating and Shucking Contest

The Louisiana Oyster Festival attracts thousands of visitors to this small community on Bayou LaFourche to enjoy Cajun music, food and fun. Featured events at the festival are the competition for the World's Champion Oyster Eater, the Oyster Shucking Contest and the election of an oyster king.

Time: 2nd weekend in July.
Place: South LaFourche High School, MS 308.
Contact: (504) 632-5804

Grand Chenier

Rockefeller Wildlife Refuge

A variety of wildlife, from ducks, coots and geese to muskrats, raccoons and alligators frequent this 84,000-acre refuge. Visit the research areas and display pens for close-up views of animals, or drive the shell-surfaced roads to take your chances at glimpsing them in the wild.

Time: Mar. 1-Dec. 31.
Place: SE of town on MS 82.
Contact: (318) 538-2165

Grand Coteau

Antebellum Girls' School

Founded in 1921, this girls' school is the oldest Sacred Heart School still in continuous operation in North America. The three-storey main building was built in 1831 and is one of several antebellum structures on campus. Other special attractions include an ancient oak alley and formal garden.

Place: On Church St. just off LA 93.

Grand Isle

Find a Brown Pelican

The Brown Pelican, Louisiana's state bird, is endangered elsewhere but can be found in abundance at Grand Isle and elsewhere along the Gulf Coast.
Place: Ask locally for directions.

View of Oil Rigs

One of the benefits of a drive along the Gulf is a good view of many off-shore oil rigs. One particularly good stretch follows along the coast on LA 1. The portion that passes Grand Isle features a sandy beach.

Holly Beach

Songbird Watching

The community of Holly Beach sits amidst 26 miles of Gulf Beach and features swimming, sunbathing and picnicking facilities. Birdwatching is great all year, but is particularly appealing in February, when warblers and other songbirds migrate northward from Mexico and the Yucatan.
Contact: (504) 568-5854 or 5859

Sabine Wildlife Reserve

Alligators, red foxes and other wildlife are abundant year-round in this 142,846-acre area of brackish and fresh water pools. The reserve also serves as a wintering spot for blue and snow geese. A marsh trail is maintained to provide access by foot into the wilderness areas.
Time: Mon.-Fri., 7 a.m.-3:30 p.m.
Contact: (504) 568-5854 or 5859

Houma

Shrimp Packing Plants

The Houma area has two shrimp plants that give special tours. You can see people packing shrimp or other types of fish, depending on the season. Be sure to call ahead and make an appointment.
Time: Mon.-Fri., 8:30 a.m.-4 p.m., by appt. only.
Place: A.C.L.I. Shrimp Plant and Indian Ridge Shrimp Company, 12 mi. S of town on LA 56.
Contact: A.C.L.I. Shrimp Plant: (504) 594-5869. Indian Ridge Shrimp Company: (504) 594-3361.

Sugar Cane Plant

The US Sugar Cane Experimental Plant offers tours of their facilities, including a greenhouse with 30-foot tall sugar cane plants. You can see many varieties of the plants at

LOUISIANA

Houma

each stage of their growth. You must call ahead and make an appointment.

Time: Mon.-Fri., 8:30 a.m.-4 p.m., by appt. only.
Place: Off LA 311 on Little Bayou Black Dr.
Contact: (504) 872-6326

Jennings

Zigler Art Museum

Housed in a beautiful colonial-style home, the Zigler Museum features an outstanding collection of European and American paintings and a series of exceptional dioramas of Louisiana wildlife scenes. A special attraction is the Louisiana Gallery, where works by the state's best-known artists are displayed.

Time: Tues.-Fri., 10 a.m.-noon and 2-5 p.m.; Sat.-Sun., 2-5 p.m.
Place: 411 Clara St.
Contact: (318) 824-0114

Lafayette

Thoroughbred Racing

Situated on the banks of the Vermillion River, Lafayette was founded in 1823 by French Acadians from Nova Scotia. It is particularly scenic during

March when azalea trees are in bloom. Exciting thoroughbred races are held at Evangeline Downs. Check locally for schedule.

Time: Races: late Apr.-early Sept.
Place: Races: US 167.
Contact: (318) 233-2705

The Mini-Swamp

Alligators, swans and frogs inhabit a moss-shrouded miniature swamp built into the center of the University of Southern Louisiana campus. You can get close enough to the alligators to take a picture without any danger. The next best thing to the Everglades!

Place: On campus of University of Southern Louisiana, off Hebard St.
Contact: (318) 264-6000

Lake Charles

Lake Charles Beach

One of the most appealing stops along Lakeshore Drive and I-10 is the Lake Charles Beach on the north shore of Lake Charles. It features bathhouses, easy parking and a scenic view of the lake.

Many

Hodges Gardens

This 4,700-acre "garden in the forest" puts on a special Christmas light display during the month of December. You can see hundreds of lights around the large lake in the gardens, a Santa Claus house and a manger scene.

Time: Early Dec., Mon.-Sun., 5-9 p.m.
Place: S of Many and N of Leesville on US 171.
Contact: (318) 586-3523
Note: Be sure to call ahead and confirm the dates of the Christmas display; during the rest of the year, there is an admission charge.

Monroe

Louisiana Purchase Garden and Zoo

This dazzling 140-acre garden features a unique combination

of more than 8,000 plants and some 850 animals in their natural habitat. Amidst the formal gardens, towering live oaks, winding waterways and animal dwellings, you'll find picnic areas and quiet scenic spots.

Time: Mon.-Sun., 8 a.m.-5 p.m.
Contact: (318) 322-2479
Note: A small admission is charged to enter the zoo.

Masur Museum of Art

A rare, comprehensive insight into the world of art is presented by this museum in northeast Louisiana. Each month a different exhibit is on display and the motifs and media used by the artist are introduced to the public through demonstrations and art classes.

Place: 1400 S. Grand St.
Contact: (318) 388-0191

Old and Rare Bibles

The Bible Research Center is a unique museum that contains a collection of early and rare Bibles and non-denominational facilities for Bible research. Also on display are engravings, maps, portraits and musical instruments dating back many centuries. Don't miss the Elsong Gardens.

Time: Mon.-Thurs., 9 a.m.-noon and 1-4:30 p.m.; other days,

by appt. Closed in Aug.
Contact: (318) 387-5281

Morgan City

Brownwell Carillon Tower

Located in scenic Brownwell Park amidst cypress trees on the shore of Lake Palourde, the carillon tower features huge bells that chime delightful melodies for picnickers and other visitors.

Time: 9 a.m.-4 p.m.
Place: N of town on LA 70 at Lake Palourde.

Natchitoches

National Fish Hatchery Aquarium

This aquarium features 20 tanks of native Louisiana fish, turtles and alligators.

Time: 8 a.m.-4 p.m.
Place: Hwy. 1.
Contact: (318) 352-5324

New Iberia

Statue of Hadrian

A seven-foot marble statue of the Emperor Hadrian, who ruled the Roman Empire from 117 to 138 A.D. It was created

in his lifetime and he probably stood for the sculptor.

Place: Corner of Weeks and St. Peter Sts.
Contact: Iberia Savings & Loan, 301 E. Peter St.

A Spicy Attraction

Spice up your visit to Louisiana with a guided tour of the McIlhenny Co., makers of Tabasco pepper sauce.

Time: Mon.-Fri., 8 a.m.-3 p.m.
Place: Avery Island.
Contact: (318) 365-8173

New Orleans

Old Absinthe House

Built sometime between 1798 and 1806, this Bourbon Street barroom has become one of the best-known establishments in the French Quarter. Its most unique feature is the absinthe frappe behind its marble-topped bar.

Place: 240 Bourbon St.

Brewery Tour

A guided tour of the Falstaff Brewing Co. offers a chance to see how grain and hops are brewed into beer. You're invited to sample the results.

Time: Mon.-Sat., 10 a.m.-2 p.m. (call first).
Place: 2601 Gravier St.
Contact: (504) 522-2000

LOUISIANA

New Orleans

Photogenic Cathedral

Built in 1794, the Cathedral of St. Louis King of France is the oldest active cathedral and one of the most photographed churches in the United States. Despite a remodeling in 1851, it retains many of its original features, including triple spires that dominate the facade of the building. Guided tours through this historic basilica take you past magnificent paintings and into a notorious dueling garden.
Time: Tours: Mon.-Sat., 9 a.m.-5 p.m.; Sun., 1-5 p.m. Sun. Masses: 6:30, 8, 9, 10 and 11 a.m.; noon and 6 p.m.
Place: On Chartes St. facing Jackson Sq.
Contact: (504) 525-9585

500 Antique Dolls

Doll lovers will be delighted by the display of more than 500 antique costumed dolls from around the world at Cabrini Children's Museum.
Time: Mon.-Fri., 10 a.m.-5 p.m.; Sat., 9 a.m.-2 p.m.
Place: 1218 Burgundy St.
Contact: (504) 586-5204

Historic Collection

This excellent collection of historic Louisiana artifacts includes rare prints, paintings and documents. It is located in a home built in 1792 and furnished with fine antiques.
Time: Tues.-Sat., 10 a.m.-4:45 p.m.
Place: 533 Royal St.
Contact: (504) 523-7146
Note: Downstairs gallery is free, but there is an admission charge for a home tour and the 10 upstairs galleries.

US Customs House

This handsome old building, built in 1848, was used as headquarters by General Butler during Union occupation after 1862. It still contains some Customs Service offices and other federal offices. Note the exterior of the building, made of a modified Egyptian motif, and the Marble Hall on the second floor, which is surrounded by 14 Corinthian marble columns 58 feet high.
Time: Mon.-Fri., 9 a.m.-5 p.m.
Place: 423 Canal St.
Contact: (504) 589-2917

French Market

If you're hankering for a tasty late night snack or a sampling of New Orleans' French tradition, a visit to the famous French Market will fill the bill. Built in the early 1800s, the market has recently been restored into a complex of shops, cafes, lounges and restaurants open around-the-clock. In addi-tion, the century-old vegetable market is still in operation. The Market's "Café Du Monde" is a popular coffee stand specializing in inexpensive café au lait and square-shaped doughnuts known as Beignets.
Place: 800-1000 blocks of Decatur St.

French Quarter Walking Tours

For a close-up view of the most picturesque Old World shops and buildings in New Orleans, try a walking tour through the famous French Quarter (called the Vieux Carré or Old Square). Originally laid out in a grid-iron plan in 1721, it features a wide range of shops, restaurants and entertainment spots. You can pick up a free brochure about self-guided walking tours of the area at the contact listed below.
Time: Mon.-Sun., 9 a.m.-5 p.m.
Contact: Greater New Orleans Tourist & Convention Commission, 334 Royal St., New Orleans, LA 70130; (504) 566-5011 or 5031.

Jackson Square

Located in the heart of the French Quarter, Jackson Square is a handsome garden park where early New Orleans welcomed heroes and held public meetings and celebrations. The focal point of the park is an equestrian bronze statue of Andrew Jackson. Besides being the historic center of the city, Jackson Square is the Quarter's unofficial Left Bank, where sidewalk artists set up shop.

Time: 8 a.m.-7 p.m.
Contact: (504) 566-5011 or 5031

Mardi Gras

The New Orleans Mardi Gras is perhaps the most famous celebration in the United States. Staged by 60 secret societies called "Krews," the gala festival begins in early February, two weeks *before* Shrove Tuesday. It includes 30 parades, several private costume balls and many hours of street dancing, masquerading and revelry. The height of the celebration comes during the weekend closest to Shrove Tuesday. With its resemblance to the seasonal festivals of ancient Rome, Mardi Gras is a fitting climax to New Orlean's carnival season, which begins January 6.

Contact: (504) 566-5011 or 5031

Space Shuttle

For a trip that's "out of this world," take a tour through the 43-acre Michoud Assembly Facility. You can see workers assembling the Space Shuttle external fuel tanks. As you enter the facility, you'll walk by a huge Saturn rocket booster. Be sure to call ahead for an appointment; they prefer visitors on Tuesdays and Thursdays.

Time: Mon.-Fri., 7:30 a.m.-4 p.m.
Place: 15 miles E of town on US 90, at 13800 Old Gentilly Rd.
Contact: (504) 255-3788
Note: Picture-taking is not allowed.

Panorama

A spectacular panoramic view of the city awaits visitors at the Top of the Mart, the world's largest revolving lounge, located in the International Trade Mart Building.

You can hear some free music there on Monday through Saturday evenings.

Time: Mon.-Fri., 10 a.m.-2 p.m.; Sat., 11 a.m.-3 a.m.; Sun., 4 p.m.-midnight.
Place: No. 2 Canal St., at the Mississippi River.
Contact: (504) 522-9795

Ferry Ride

Take a free ride on a ferry across the Mississippi River! You can board this ferry at the foot of Canal Street; in 5 minutes you'll be on the other side of the river at Algiers. If you'd like to take some time and wander around on the river bank, you can make the return trip at any time.

Time: Mon.-Sun., 6 a.m.-10:30 p.m., on the hour and the half hour from Canal St.
Place: Foot of Canal St.
Contact: (504) 361-6565

Wildlife Museum

Headquartered in the Louisiana Wildlife and Fisheries Commission building in the French Quarter, this museum features displays of hundreds of mounted birds, mammals and reptiles arranged realistically in habitat groups.

Time: Mon.-Fri., 8:30 a.m.-5:45 p.m.
Place: 400 Royal St.
Contact: (545) 568-5855

LOUISIANA

Oak Grove

Centuries-Old Live Oaks

The Oak Grove area features an abundance of "cheniers"—ridges of high ground in the marshland that support centuries-old live oaks and shelter many types of wildlife.
Place: Ask locally for directions.

Rayne

Frog Festival

Rayne stages the most spectacular frog festival in the country. Highlights of this tribute to Louisiana's long-legged swamp dweller include frog catching, cooking and eating contests, and a three-jump event where frogs are spurred on by female frog jockeys.
Time: 3rd week in Sept.
Contact: (318) 334-2332

St. Francisville

Gallery for the Birds

The Audubon Art Gallery in St. Francisville features a complete collection of 435 life-size bird portraits by John James Audubon. Audubon painted 75 of his world-famous "Birds of America" portraits in this gallery during the 1820s.
Time: 24 hours a day.
Place: St. Francisville Holiday Inn, US 61 and LA 10.
Contact: (504) 635-3821

St. Martinville

Old Church

This colorful town was founded in about 1760 by a group of French settlers, the Acadians, who were driven from Nova Scotia by the British. St. Martin's Church dates back to 1832 and may contain parts of an earlier structure built in 1765. On display inside are a Baptismal font reportedly bestowed by Louis XVI during the French Revolution and a replica of the Lourdes grotto.
Place: Main St.
Contact: (318) 394-6021

The Evangeline Oak

The legendary Evangeline Oak is said to be the place where Henry Wadsworth Longfellow's heroine, Evangeline, docked her boat at the completion of her long journey from Nova Scotia.
Place: On Port St. at Bayou Teche.

Pepper Making

Tour Evangeline Pepper Products and get a close-up look at the art of making pepper and other seasoning condiments.
Time: Mon.-Fri., 8 a.m.-5 p.m.
Place: Banker Rd.
Contact: (318) 394-3091

Shreveport

Barbershop Singing

You won't want to miss the melodious harmonies of the S.P.E.B.S.Q.S.A.—the Society for the Preservation and Encouragement of Barbershop Quartet Singing in America. Local chapter meetings give you a free concert—so plan to come and croon!
Contact: Mike McClallen; (318) 456-2224 or 456-3213. Call for current meeting times and places.

Barnwell Garden and Art Center

The Center's beautiful, 7,850-square foot domed botanical conservatory contains an abundance of native and tropical flowers and plants. The gallery nearby houses numerous art exhibits and offers a panoramic view of the Red River.

Time: Mon.-Fri., 9 a.m.-4:30 p.m.; Sat.-Sun., 1-5 p.m.
Place: 501 Fant Pkwy.
Contact: (318) 226-6495

Meadows Museum of Indochinese Art

The Algur Meadows Museum houses the complete collection of oils and sketches created by Jean Despujois during his 20-month journey through French Indochina in 1936-37.

Time: Tues.-Fri., 1-5 p.m.; Sat.-Sun., 2-5 p.m.
Place: Administration Building of Centenary College, Centenary Blvd., one block N of King's Hwy.
Contact: (318) 869-5169

American Rose Society Gardens

Rustic pathways meandering beneath towering pines lead to a 118-acre garden where roses bloom from April through December and a multitude of other flowers and plants blossom all year. A carillon tower provides delightful music. America's largest plant society is headquartered here and keeps track of all old and new varieties of roses.

Time: Mid-Apr.-mid-Sept., Mon.-Fri., 8:30 a.m.-4:30 p.m.; Sat.-Sun., 8:30 a.m.-8 p.m. Mid-Sept.-mid-Apr., Mon.-Fri., 8:30 a.m.-4:30 p.m.
Place: Take I-20 W of Shreveport and E of Greenwood, then N on US 79/80, left on Jefferson-Paige Rd.
Contact: (318) 938-5402

Norton Art Gallery

Located in a wooded, 40-acre landscaped park, this gallery is one of Shreveport's major cultural attractions. Incomparable collections of American and European paintings, sculptures and decorative arts spanning the past four centuries are housed in its 13 galleries. Two collections of western art by Frederic Remington and Charles M. Russell are on permanent display.

Time: Tues.-Sun., 1-5 p.m.
Place: 4747 Creswell Ave.
Contact: (318) 863-4201

Sulphur

Brimstone Museum

An old railroad station is home for this museum, which features films and exhibits on the history of the sulphur industry as well as other memorabilia of southwest Louisiana.

Time: Mon.-Fri., 9 a.m.-2 p.m.
Place: 800 Picard Rd., in Frasch Park.
Contact: (318) 527-7142

Creole Nature Trail

Starting in Sulphur, the Creole Trail winds through marshlands, swamplands and along the Gulf Coast. Take this scenic route past a wide variety of land-types and wildlife.

Place: Jct. of LA 27 and LA 82.
Contact: (318) 527-7142

Ville Platte

Louisiana State Arboretum

These 301 acres of natural beauty are located on the outskirts of Chicot State Park on sparkling Lake Chicot. Nature trails lead past more than 100 species of plant life native to Louisiana. Plants are labeled for easy identification and a guidebook, available at the park, displays characteristics of trees and plants.

Time: 8 a.m.-6 p.m.
Place: NW of town on LA 3042.
Contact: (318) 363-2403

Ville Platte

Jousting Contest

One of the highlights of the annual Louisiana Cotton Festival is the "Tournoi," an exciting jousting tournament. Young men clad in the costumes of medieval knighthood circle a track on horseback, aiming their lances at two-inch rings that represent enemies of the cotton industry, such as the boll weevil or synthetic fabrics. He who spears the most is the hero of the season.

Time: 2nd week of Oct.
Contact: (318) 363-1878

MISSISSIPPI

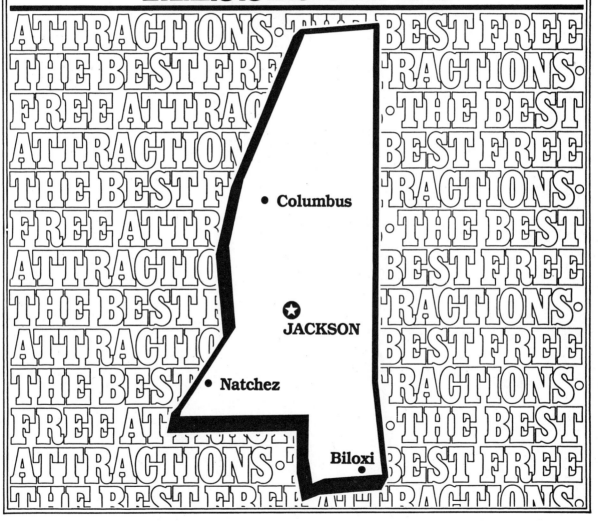

• Columbus

✪ JACKSON

• Natchez

Biloxi •

MISSISSIPPI

Belzoni

Oriental Chickens

A stop at Wister Gardens is sure to burn up some of your photo budget. This colorful 14-acre garden contains 8,000 azaleas, 1,000 roses, 5,000 tulips and 750 chrysanthemums, as well as an array of swans, flamingos, ducks and oriental chickens.

Time: 8 a.m.-5 p.m.
Contact: (601) 247-3025

Biloxi

County Beach

Biloxi nestles up to the Harrison County Sand Beach, 26 miles long and up to 300 feet wide. You can't see the sand for the people from Memorial Day to Labor Day, but in a good year the beach is enjoyable from late March to mid-October.

Contact: (601) 374-2717

Shrimp Festival

Each year, Biloxi celebrates the coming of the shrimp season with a gala festival that includes a colorful boat parade, Cajun cooking, music, Fais-Do-Do dancing, pageantry and revelry. During the Blessing of the Fleet, each of the boats in pro-

cession is blessed by a priest as they pass by him.

Time: Late spring or early summer. Blessing: 1st Sun. in June.
Place: Blessing: Small Craft Harbor, on US 90 on the E edge of town.
Contact: (601) 374-2717

Kessler Air Force Base

Kessler Air Force Base is the electronics training center for the Air Force and home of the Hurricane Hunters. It features exhibits of aircraft and base history.

Time: Mon.-Fri., 8 a.m.-4 p.m.; Sat., by appt.

Place: George White Ave., off MS 90.
Contact: (601) 377-3504

Live Coastal Zone Animals

Displays of live coastal zone animals including fish, reptiles, amphibians and invertebrates are featured. Colorful films are available for viewing.

Time: Mon.-Fri., 8 a.m.-5 p.m.; Sat., 8 a.m.-1 p.m.
Place: Marine Education Center, MS 90, East Beach.
Contact: (601) 435-3095

Forest

Bienville National Forest

This dense pine and hardwood forest covers 170,000 acres in central Mississippi. Special features include the Bienville Pines Scenic Area, noted for its nature trail in a stand of virgin pine, and the Shockaloo National Recreation Trail—23 miles of hiking trails.

Place: Bienville Pines Scenic Area: 1 mi. S of town on MS 501. Shockaloo Trail: 5 mi. W of town on US 80.
Contact: (601) 847-1725

Gautier

Singing River

Legend goes that this mysterious sound is the echo of a chant sung by an Indian tribe that was pushed into the Pascagoula River long ago. The unexplained low buzzing melody that works its way along the river, especially during August, September and October evenings, has mystified visitors for ages. You can hear the singing river from its shore.
Place: Off Rte. 90.
Contact: (601) 762-3391

Hattiesburg

DeSoto National Forest

This sprawling, southeastern Mississippi forest spreads across 501,200 acres from Laurel to the Gulf of Mexico near Biloxi. It features picnicking, camping and swimming in 11 developed recreation areas. A 50-mile float trip on Black and Beaverdam Creeks offers an intimate view of scenic streams. The W. W. Ashe Nursery in nearby Brooklyn is one of the largest US Forest Service tree nurseries in the nation.
Time: 9 a.m.-5 p.m.
Place: 10 mi. SE of town on US 49.
Contact: (601) 545-3300; Nursery: (601) 582-7721.

Holly Springs

Kate Freeman Clark Art Gallery

Reportedly the only art gallery of its kind in the world, this unique exhibit hall features the largest single collection of paintings by a single artist housed anywhere.
Time: By appt.
Place: College Ave.
Contact: (601) 252-2511

Jackson

Governor's Mansion

The Mississippi Governor's Mansion, which occupies an entire block of East Capitol Street, is the second oldest executive mansion in the US, having been the home of 35 state governors since 1842. It is one of the few structures to survive Jackson's frequent burnings during the Civil War. The outside of the mansion bears an uncanny resemblance to the White House; it contains rooms and furnishings appropriate to the 1850s.
Time: Tues.-Fri., 9:30-11:30 a.m. (groups should call ahead).
Place: Capitol St. between N. Congress and N. West Sts.
Contact: (601) 354-7650

Mississippi Museum of Natural Science

Outdoor lovers will enjoy the museum's 25,000 specimens of state animals, birds, fishes, fossils and vertebrates. Tour of the museum includes a 30-minute film on the environment and endangered species.
Time: Mon.-Fri., 8 a.m.-5 p.m.; Sat., 9 a.m.-5 p.m.
Place: 111 N. Jefferson.
Contact: (601) 354-7303

New State Capitol

This 78-year-old building resembles the national Capitol and is one of the most architecturally prominent structures in the South. A golden eagle rests on the center of the Capitol's three domes. A tour of the edifice includes visits to the governor's office and legislative meeting rooms.
Time: Mon.-Fri., 8 a.m.-5 p.m.; Sat., 9:30 a.m.-4:30 p.m.
Place: High St.
Contact: (601) 354-7294

MISSISSIPPI

Jackson

Old Capitol

A stunning example of Greek Revival architecture, this building was used as the state's Capitol from 1839 to 1903. Portions of its interior have been restored. Other rooms contain exhibits of Mississippi's history.
Time: May-Oct., Tues.-Sat., 9:30 a.m.-4:30 p.m.; Sun., 1-5 p.m.
Place: 100 State St.
Contact: (601) 354-6222

Municipal Art Gallery

Housed in an 1850s antebellum home, this gallery contains changing exhibits in a variety of mediums by local artists.
Time: Sept.-July, Tues.-Sat., 9 a.m.-5 p.m.; Sun., 2-5 p.m. Closed Mon.
Place: 839 N. State St.
Contact: (601) 352-0128

City Hall

Jackson City Hall, built in 1846, is one of the few antebellum structures remaining after Jackson was burned by General Sherman during the Civil War. Visit the Josh Holbert garden with the statue honoring the city's namesake, Andrew Jackson, as well.
Time: Mon.-Fri., 8 a.m.-5 p.m.; other hours by appt.
Contact: (601) 960-1000

Neon Light Sculptures

The Mississippi Museum of Art in the Art Center features a noted collection of paintings, ceramics, sculpture, photography, glassware and even neon light sculptures. Additional exhibits on loan contribute to the variety of subjects displayed.
Time: Tues. and Fri., 10 a.m.-10 p.m.; Wed. and Thurs., 10 a.m.-6 p.m.; Sat., 10 a.m.-6 p.m.; Sun., 1-5 p.m.
Place: 201 E. Pascagoula.
Contact: (601) 354-3538

Military History in 3-D

A special attraction of the Mississippi Military Museum is a vivid, 3-D presentation of US military history from the Spanish-American War to Vietnam with special emphasis on the combat experiences of Mississippians.
Time: Mon.-Fri., 9 a.m.-4:30 p.m.
Place: War Memorial Bldg., 120 N. State St.
Contact: (601) 354-7207

Laurel

Varied Treasures

Housed in a 60-year-old Georgian-style building, the Lauren Rogers Library and Museum of Art contains an outstanding collection of books, manuscripts, furnishings and relics. Special highlights are the works of such well-known artists as Rembrandt, Bellows, Homer, Whistler and Constable. The museum also features Georgian silver and basket collections, European and Oriental paintings, and Indian artifacts.
Time: Tues.-Sat., 10 a.m.-noon and 1-5 p.m.; Sun., 2-5 p.m.
Place: Fifth and Seventh Sts.
Contact: (601) 428-4875

Lorman

Old Country Store

Old-fashioned charm mixed with genuine customer service give this unique store a character all its own. Founded in 1875, it is believed to be one of the oldest continuously-operating general merchandise stores in the nation. Many of its original fixtures, including an antique cheese cutter and wind-up shoe display rack, are still in use. In addition, an adjoining museum contains numerous mementos of the country-store era.
Time: Mon.-Sat., 8:30 a.m.-6 p.m.; Sun., noon-6 p.m.
Place: 11 mi. S of town on US 61.
Contact: (601) 437-3661

Merigold

Rushing Winery

This is the first winery in Mississippi since Prohibition. It features 25 acres of vineyards and a tasting room furnished in antiques. An informative 30 to 45 minute tour is available.

Time: Tues.-Sat., 8 a.m.-5 p.m. (Best to call ahead.)
Place: S of town on US 61; watch for sign.
Contact: (601) 748-2731

Natchez

Grand Village of the Natchez

Situated amidst 80 acres of nature trails and mounds, the Natchez Indian visitor center includes a museum with artifacts, burial mounds, a gift shop and a 60-seat auditorium where a 15-minute film is presented.

Time: Mon.-Sat., 9 a.m.-5 p.m.; Sun., 1:30-5 p.m.
Place: 400 Jefferson Davis Blvd.
Contact: (601) 445-6502

Mammy's Cupboard Restaurant

This unique roadside restaurant is actually built in the shape of a mammy, 28 feet tall with a five-foot chain necklace and horseshoes for earrings. View this example of roadside America, or, if you're hungry, get a dinner—the specialty is tender fried chicken served with home-cut French fries and pre-sweetened tea.

Time: Restaurant: Mon.-Sat., 8 a.m.-7 p.m.
Place: Rte. 61 S of Natchez.
Contact: (601) 442-9554

Walking Tour

Established in 1716 on the bluffs of the Mississippi River, the city of Natchez is one of the oldest communities in North America. It is built on the site of an ancient Indian village. One of the best ways to view the historic buildings and tree-lined streets that depict Natchez's heritage is to take a free, self-conducted walking tour. Ask the contact for details on arrangements.

Time: Tours: year-round.
Contact: Natchez-Adams County Chamber of Commerce, Jefferson and Commerce Sts.; (601) 445-4611.

Oxford

Rowan Oak— Faulkner Country

This antebellum home, built about 1840, was the home of author William Faulkner from 1930 to 1962. It is preserved exactly as it was in Faulkner's time and contains many of his personal effects. The home remains as inaccessible as Faulkner would have wanted, but once you find it, graduate students staying there will be glad to show you around.

Time: Mon.-Fri., 10 a.m.-noon and 2-4 p.m.; Sat., 10 a.m.-noon; by appt. for groups of 10 or more.
Place: Old Taylor Rd.
Contact: (601) 234-3284

University Museums

Among the highlights on the tree-lined University of Mississippi campus are several fine museums. You can see collections ranging from Greek and Roman antiquities to natural science instruments. Excellent student and traveling art exhibits are featured in the University Gallery, as well.

Time: Museums: Tues.-Sat., 10 a.m.-4 p.m.; Sun., 1-4 p.m.
Place: Museums: University and Fifth, University of Mississippi campus. Gallery: Fine Arts Center, University of Mississippi campus.
Contact: Museums: (601) 232-7073. Gallery: (601) 232-7193.

MISSISSIPPI

Oxford

Mississippi Literati

The Department of Archives and Special Collections in the University of Mississippi Library contains a well-known collection of works by and about such famous Mississippi authors as William Faulkner, Eudora Welty, Tennessee Williams and Richard Wright. Also featured is an excellent collection of recorded blues music.

Time: Mon.-Thurs., 8:30 a.m.-8 p.m.; Fri., 8:30 a.m.-5 p.m.; Sat., 9 a.m.-noon.
Place: John Davis Williams Library, University of Mississippi campus.
Contact: (601) 232-7408

Philadelphia

Swinging Bridge

Visit Nanih Waiya Historic Site, the legendary birthplace of the Choctaw Indians and site of their Sacred Mound. A unique feature of the site is a swinging bridge leading to a cave under the mound. Graphic explanations of the legend concerning the mound and cave are provided. Enjoy the picnic area and shelter, a nature trail, primitive camping and an activity building. Each July, the Choctaws celebrate their customs at the Choctaw Indian Fair in this area.

Contact: (601) 656-1742
Time: Fair: Mid-July, Wed.-Sun. Historic site: open year-round.
Place: 20 mi. NE of town on MS 21, in Nanih Waiya State Park.

Picayune

Space Shuttle Testing Site

Located here is the space shuttle main engine testing site and the former testing site of Apollo/Saturn V rocket boosters used in the manned Lunar Landing Program. Research conducted includes application of space technology to problems on earth.

Time: Tours: Mon.-Fri., 1 p.m.
Place: NASA National Space Technology Laboratories, 13 mi. S of town via I-59, on MS 607.
Contact: (601) 688-2211

Port Gibson

Tower Climb

In Grand Gulf State Military Park you can climb the tower for a view 30 miles in each

direction. The park offers picnic areas on the banks of the Mississippi, a cemetery where you can take rubbings and a museum with a small gun collection. The park is also restoring carriages to add to the small number it already has on display. Note that little remains of the original fortifications.

Time: Park: 7 a.m.-8 p.m. Museum: Tues.-Sat., 8 a.m.-5 p.m., Sun., 10 a.m.-6 p.m.
Place: 10 mi. NW of town off US 61.
Contact: (601) 437-5911

Ridgeland

Mississippi Crafts Center

This dogtrot cabin reproduction contains the home of the Mississippi Craftsmen's Guild. Crafts demonstrations are free and worth stopping to see, and if you're in the mood to buy, the products are for sale.

Time: 9 a.m.-5 p.m. Demonstrations: Mar.-Sept., Sat., Sun., Wed. (times are variable, so check with contact).
Contact: (601) 856-7546

Tupelo

Mount Locust

The only remaining inn of the 50 that existed along the Natchez Trace, Mount Locust has been restored to its early 19th-century glory. A living history program is conducted inside.

Time: Living history: Feb.-Nov., 8:30 a.m.-5:30 p.m. Grounds open year-round.
Place: 15 mi NE of town on Natchez Trace Pkwy.
Contact: (601) 445-4211

Scenic Drive

One of several visitor centers and museums along the historic 300-mile Natchez Trace Parkway, the Tupelo Visitors Center houses a small museum containing items relating to the Trace's history. Nature trails are nearby for those who want a scenic hike.

Time: 8 a.m.-5 p.m., closed Christmas.
Place: At the entrance to the Natchez Trace Parkway.
Contact: (601) 842-1572
Note: The Trace is not open to commercial vehicles. Tour buses are allowed if previous notice is given.

Vicksburg

Vicksburg National Military Park

Bordering the eastern and northern ends of the city, this park covers more than 1,700 acres and marks the site of the historic Battle of Vicksburg in 1863. Museum exhibits and graphic displays along a 16-mile route through the park vividly depict the history of the famous Civil War battle. The visitor center at the park entrance is an excellent starting place for a tour.

Time: June-Aug., 7 a.m.-7 p.m.; rest of year, 8 a.m.-5 p.m.
Contact: (601) 636-0583

Miniature Atomic Blasts

Atomic blasts and floods, all in miniature, of course, are likely to greet you on a tour of this US Army Corps of Engineers research and testing laboratory. Main fields of research range from hydraulics and nuclear explosives to environmental relationships. River, harbor and flood control projects are studied on scale models.

Time: Mon.-Fri., 7:45 a.m.-4:15 p.m. Guided tours: 10 a.m. and 2 p.m.
Place: Halls Ferry Rd.
Contact: (601) 636-3111, ext. 2502

Washington

Aaron Burr's Arraignment

The Jefferson College campus is one of the most historic sites in the state. Here the first Mississippi State Constitution was written in 1817, Aaron Burr was arraigned for treason and Jefferson Davis attended school. The two main buildings have been restored to their 1840 elegance. Visit the museum of early Mississippi history, and enjoy the nature trails and picnic facilities.

Time: Mon.-Sat., 9 a.m.-5 p.m.; Sun., 1-5 p.m. Grounds: dawn-dusk.
Place: 3 mi. E of town on US 61.
Contact: (601) 442-2901

MISSISSIPPI

Yazoo City

Triangle Cultural Center

This well-known cultural center is the home of the popular Playhouse 75 and also houses a craft shop.

Time: Mon.-Fri., 8 a.m.-5 p.m. By appt. for other hours.
Contact: (601) 746-2273

NORTH CAROLINA

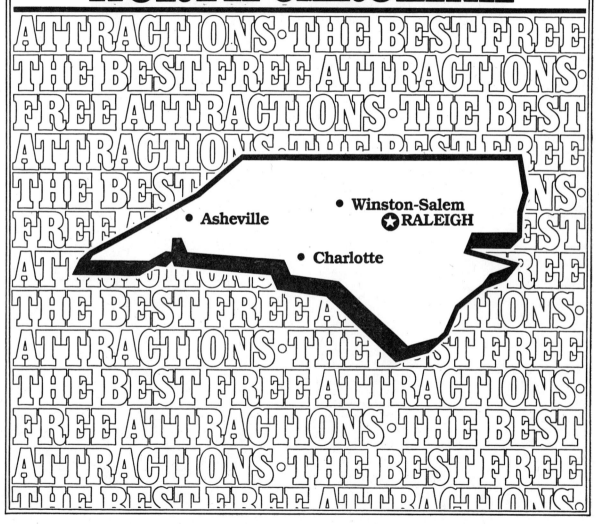

ATTRACTIONS · THE BEST FREE
THE BEST FREE ATTRACTIONS ·
FREE ATTRACTIONS · THE BEST
ATTRACTIONS · THE BEST FREE
THE BEST FREE ATTRACTIONS ·
FREE ATTRACTIONS · THE BEST
ATTRACTIONS · THE BEST FREE
THE BEST FREE ATTRACTIONS ·
ATTRACTIONS · THE BEST FREE
THE BEST FREE ATTRACTIONS ·
FREE ATTRACTIONS · THE BEST
ATTRACTIONS · THE BEST FREE
THE BEST FREE ATTRACTIONS ·

- Asheville
- Winston-Salem
- ★ RALEIGH
- Charlotte

NORTH CAROLINA

Asheville

Armor Collection

The Smithsonian would like to own the Van Sant Armor Collection, but so far it remains in Asheville. The museum is stocked with entire outfits of armor as well as weapons and shields.

Time: Tues.-Fri., 10 a.m.-5 p.m.; Sat.-Sun., 1-5 p.m.
Place: Asheville Art Museum, Lower Level, Civic Center Complex.
Contact: (704) 253-3227

Shakespeare in the Plaza

During the summer you can watch free performances of Shakespeare simply by showing up at the City County Plaza!

Time: July and Aug.
Place: City County Plaza.
Contact: (704) 258-5222

Rockhounders' Stop-Off

Gemstones and minerals typical of the southern Appalachian region are displayed in the Colburn Mineral Museum. Here you'll be primed with information on rockhounding in the area. On some occasions you'll even be given free sam-

ples of what to look for.

Time: Tues.-Fri., 10 a.m.-5 p.m.; Sat.-Sun., 1-5 p.m.
Place: Lower level of Thomas Wolfe Auditorium in the Civic Center Complex.
Contact: (704) 254-7162

River Week Festival

Getting to know the French Broad River is the theme of this week-long festival. It includes rafting and river hikes, some of which are guided and free. For others there's a small charge.

Time: Late Sept.
Contact: Land-of-Sky Regional Council, P.O. Box 2175, Asheville, NC 28802; (704) 254-8131.

Folk Art

At the Folk Art Center of the Southern Highland Handicraft Guild you'll discover authentic mountain crafts, including dolls, dulcimers and pottery. Craftsmen are often at work displaying skills typical of the region. There are films, folk dances and folk musical events in the auditorium.

Time: Apr.-Dec., 9 a.m.-5 p.m.; Jan.-Mar., 10 a.m.-5 p.m.
Place: E of town at Milepost 382 of the Blue Ridge Pkwy., .5 mi. N of US 70.
Contact: (704) 298-7928

Mountain Hikes

Pick up a free trail map from the Chamber of Commerce and join the Carolina Mountain Club for weekly hikes. It meets at the downtown post office on Sundays at 8 a.m. and 2 p.m.

Time: May-Oct., 8 a.m.-7 p.m.; rest of year, 8:30 a.m.-5:30 p.m.
Place: 151 Haywood St.
Contact: (704) 258-5222

Mountain Dancing

Join the Shindig-on-the-Green for square and clog dancing and listen to the plaintive ballads peculiar to the southern Appalachia area—a must!

Time: July-Aug., Sat. night.
Place: City County Plaza.
Contact: (704) 258-5222

Authors' Graves

At Riverside Cemetery you'll find the graves of Tom Wolfe (1900 to 1938) and O. Henry (1862 to 1910).

Time: Sunrise to sunset.
Place: Birch St., off Pearson Dr.

Craggy Gardens

One of the area's major tourist attractions, the visual feast at Craggy Gardens reaches its peak in mid-to late-June when the rhododendrons bloom. There's a self-guided trail that passes by mountain laurel and azaleas on its way to an overlook of rocks with a magnificent view. Wonderful area for picnics and hikes.

Time: Anytime.
Place: 37 mi. N of town at mi. 363.4 of Blue Ridge Pkwy.
Contact: (704) 258-5222

Blue Ridge Parkway

Without question the Blue Ridge Parkway is one of the great scenic drives in the country. It runs for 469 miles in both Virginia and North Carolina. The route connects Shenandoah National Park in the north with Great Smoky Mountains National Park in the south. For a free map and information on the most interesting stops (including 100 overlooks), call or write the contact listed below.

Contact: Blue Ridge Pkwy. Assn., P.O. Box 475, Asheville, NC 28802; (704) 258-2850.

Antique Cars

On display in the Estes-Winn Memorial are 34 antique and vintage automobiles dating back to 1905.

Time: Apr.-Oct., 9 a.m.-4:30 p.m.
Place: Groveland Rd., near Macon Ave., 2 mi. NE of town.
Contact: (704) 253-7651

Handwoven Cloth

Biltmore Homespun Shops shows the traditional steps in

making woolen cloth—from fleece to finished product. Here ancient skills of dyeing, spinning and weaving have been preserved and can be seen on tours.

Time: Shop: Mon.-Sat., 9 a.m.-5 p.m.; Sun., 1-6 p.m. Closed Sept.-May, Sun. Tour: Apr.-Oct., Mon.-Fri., 9 a.m.-4 p.m.(closed during lunch).
Place: Off Groveland Rd., near Macon Ave., 2 mi. NE of town.
Contact: (704) 253-7651

Botanical Gardens

Stroll through these ten acres of shaded glens and peaceful pathways. View over 500 plants representing the botanical beauty of the Southern Highlands, known throughout the world for its outstanding variety of flowering shrubs and plants.

Time: Sunrise to sunset.
Place: University of North Carolina campus.
Contact: (704) 258-6600

East's Highest Peak

The view is stupendous from Mt. Mitchell, the East's highest peak (6,684 feet). The area is covered with balsam forests, and there's a 45-foot observation tower for even a better vantage point. On a clear day you can see the Great Smoky Mountains and Charlotte.

Place: 35 mi. NE of Asheville at mi. 355.4 of the Blue Ridge Pkwy. Drive via NC 128 to within 300 feet of the tower.
Contact: (704) 675-4611

Bailey

Medicinal Garden

At the Country Doctor Museum is a medicinal garden, very popular with visitors who'll find a cornucopia of healing plants represented. The museum displays every-

Bailey

thing from apothecary and leech jars to pocket spittoons.
Time: Mar.-Nov., Wed. and Sun., 2-5 p.m.
Place: On NC 264.
Contact: (919) 235-4165

Beaufort

Shelling

Primitive camping and shelling are two of the outstanding draws of Cape Lookout National Seashore, a 58-mile stretch of isolated beach along the Outer Banks.
Contact: Superintendent, Cape Lookout National Seashore, P.O. Box 690, Beaufort, NC 28516; (919) 728-2121.

Ship Models

If you're into ship models or interested in boat building, stop off at the Hampton Mariners Museum, which is rich in maritime exhibits.
Time: Mon.-Fri., 9 a.m.-5 p.m.; Sat., 10 a.m.-5 p.m.; Sun., 2-5 p.m.
Place: 120 Turner St.
Contact: (919) 728-7317

Benson

Mule Days

Mule pull-ins (testing mules' strength at pulling logs), parades, bluegrass music and clogging add up to a happy fall celebration in Benson. Thirty governors enter the Governor's Mule Race—by proxy, of course.
Time: 4th weekend in Sept.
Place: Singing Grove Park.
Contact: (919) 894-3825

Boone

Gospel Festival

"Who so ever will may come." Come along to sing at the base of the mountain in one of the region's oldest festivals (going for more than 50 years) held for one day in late June. Join gospel singers in an open-air singalong which has attracted both Oral Roberts and Billy Graham at different times.
Time: 4th Sun. in June, 9:30 a.m.-4:30 p.m.
Place: 17 mi. S of town on NC 105, then 2 mi. N on US 221.
Contact: (704) 898-4720

Brevard

Lovely Falls

The area around Brevard is noted for more than 200 waterfalls—one of the most beautiful is Looking Glass Falls. In the same location is an enormous rock formation which you may enjoy. Connestee Falls, located farther along US 276, is also a lovely site for picnicking and hiking.
Place: 8 mi. NW of town via US 276.
Contact: (704) 883-3700

Panoramic View

Mt. Pisgah, off the Blue Ridge Parkway, rises 5,749 feet. Hike the one-mile trail to its summit for one of the better views in the state.

Scenic River Drive

There's a beautiful stretch of road along the French Broad River between Brevard and Asheville that you shouldn't miss. You can see a striking series of falls and cascades along the way.
Place: N on US 276 toward Waynesville.
Contact: (704) 883-3700

Burlington

Mounted Wildlife

Mounted specimens from Africa, Alaska, India and South America are displayed at the McDade Wildlife Museum.
Time: Mon.-Fri., 8 a.m.-5 p.m.
Place: 1333 Overbrook Rd.
Contact: (919) 228-1338

Battle Film

A pre-revolutionary battle took place at what is now Alamance Battleground State Historic

Site. There are a few displays on the battle and a 25-minute show combining film and slides to fill you in on the area's historic significance.
Time: Tues.-Sat., 9 a.m.-5 p.m.; Sun., 1-5 p.m.
Place: 6 mi. SW of town on NC 62.
Contact: (919) 227-4785

Chapel Hill

Wildflowers
The North Carolina Botanical Garden is noted for its herbs

(more than a hundred), carnivorous plants and wildflowers.
Time: Mon.-Fri., 8 a.m.-5 p.m.; Sat., 10 a.m.-4 p.m.; Sun., 2-5 p.m.

Place: On Laurel Hill Rd. and US 15/501 Bypass.
Contact: (919) 967-2246

Period Room
The late 18th-century English Knapp Room and 19th-century French art (including a Delacroix) are the main draws of the Ackland Art Museum.
Time: Tues.-Sat., 10 a.m.-5 p.m.; Sun., 2-6 p.m.
Place: S. Columbia St.
Contact: (919) 966-5736

Charlotte

Gold Coins
From 1837 to 1860 a gold rush swept through this area. The Mint Museum of Art features gold coins of that era as well as ceramics, pre-Columbian pottery and paintings from the Renaissance and Baroque periods.
Time: Tues.-Fri., 10 a.m.-5 p.m.; Sat.-Sun., 2-5 p.m.
Place: 501 Hempstead Pl.
Contact: (704) 334-9723

Fashions of the Past
The Mint Museum of History features American fashions from all periods. Costumes are authentic and beautifully dislayed. Changing exhibits add

another dimension to a visit here.
Time: Tues.-Fri., 10 a.m.-5 p.m.; Sat.-Sun., 2-5 p.m.
Place: 3500 Shamrock Dr.
Contact: (704) 568-1774

Transparent Woman
Turn on the talking, transparent woman and hear her tell all about her working parts (25-minute tapes). If that's not enough, there's a snake collection and live animals, including an albino skunk!
Time: Mon.-Sat., 9 a.m.-5 p.m.; Sun., 2-5 p.m.
Place: 1658 Sterling Rd.
Contact: (704) 333-0506

Creswell

Plantation Tour
Tour Somerset Place, a 14-room plantation built in the 1830s in Greek Revival style. A good example of pre-Civil War lifestyle.
Time: Mon.-Sat., 9 a.m.-5 p.m.; Sun., 1-5 p.m.
Place: On Lake Phelps, 9 mi. S of town via US 64.
Contact: (919) 797-4560

Currie

Musket Firings
A five-minute slide program brings Moore's Creek National

NORTH CAROLINA

Currie

Military Park to life as do Sunday afternoon programs throughout the summer. These include weapons demonstrations and a typical Revolutionary War encampment.
Time: May-Oct., Mon.-Fri., 8 a.m.-5 p.m.; Sat.-Sun., 8 a.m.-6 p.m.; rest of year, 8 a.m.-5 p.m.
Place: 1 mi. W of town via NC 210.
Contact: (919) 283-5591

Durham

Tobacco Museum

The Duke family lived in this historic home, built in 1852. It has been beautifully restored and is the only tobacco museum in the state. A 22-minute film gives background information to help you appreciate the history of the home and related cigarette factories on its grounds.
Time: Tues.-Sat., 9 a.m.-5 p.m.; Sun., 1-5 p.m.
Place: Duke Homestead Rd.
Contact: (919) 477-5498

Fayetteville

Parachute Drops

Call ahead to find out the schedule of parachute drops when the 82nd Airborne Division carries out its famous training sessions. Usually, 200 men drop at a time, making a dramatic scene for spectators. Call to find the location where they'll land (it varies with weather conditions.)
Contact: Public Information Office Headquarters, 18th Airborne Corps, Fort Bragg, NC 28307; (919) 396-3625. Jump information: Mon.-Fri., (919) 396-6805; Sat.-Sun., (919) 396-6100.

Flat Rock

Carl Sandburg Home

Carl Sandburg lived in this home for the last 22 years of his life. During July and August the park staff presents programs based on the late author's works. Call for dates and times, which vary each year.
Time: 9 a.m.-5 p.m.
Place: W of US 25 on Little River Rd.
Contact: (704) 693-4178

Fontana Village

TVA's Tallest Dam

Fontana Dam on the Little Tennessee River is the tallest in the TVA system. Tours include a 30-minute film on its construction and a look at three giant turbines. Particularly beautiful in the fall.
Time: Tour: 9:30 a.m-4 p.m.
Place: 2.5 mi. N of town on US 28.
Contact: (704) 498-2241

Franklin

River Gorge

The Cullasaja Gorge runs between Highlands and Franklin for 25 miles; you can follow the gorge on the Highlands Road. In this deep canyon are three photogenic falls: Bridal Veil, Dry and Cullasaja Falls—all worth stopping at. Truly one of the most beautiful areas in the state.
Contact: (704) 524-3161

Hidden Rainbows

The Franklin Gem and Mineral Museum, housed in what was once a jail, has a good collection of fossils, gems and fluorescent minerals which glow in a rainbow of colors.
Time: May-Nov., Mon.-Sat., 10 a.m.-4 p.m.
Place: 2 W. Main St.
Contact: (704) 524-3161

Gastonia

Exceptional Museum

The largest land mammal collection in North America, 6,000 mounted birds, a living farm from 1754, a nature trail with

more species of trees than you'd find in all of Europe, a grist mill grinding corn, and a planetarium—what more could you ask from the Schick Museum? One of the best!
Time: Museum: Tues.-Fri., 9 a.m.-5 p.m.; Sun., 2-5 p.m. Planetarium: Sat., 3 p.m.; Sun., 3 and 4 p.m.
Place: 1500 E. Garrison Blvd.
Contact: (704) 864-3962

Georgeville
Underground Mine
On a tour of the Reed Gold Mine State Historic Site you'll see a 20-minute film and an underground mine. In 1799 the first discovery of gold in the US occurred in this area. There's a charge for gold panning, but everything else is free.
Time: Tues.-Sat., 9 a.m.-5 p.m.; Sun., 1-5 p.m.
Place: 2 mi. S of town on Reed Mine Rd.
Contact: (704) 786-8337

Goldsboro
River Bluff
Follow a self-guided nature trail to a picturesque river bluff. The area yields fossil shells and bones.
Place: 14 mi. SE of town on NC 111.
Contact: (919) 733-4181

Greensboro
Musket Firings
In the summer months you can enjoy guided tours of Guilford Courthouse National Military Park and see musket demonstrations similar to those used during the battle of March 15, 1781. During the rest of the year, you're free to walk around the park.
Time: May-Labor Day, Mon.-Sun., 8:30 a.m.-6 p.m.; rest of year, Mon.-Sun., 8:30 a.m.-5 p.m.
Place: 1 mi. N of town, off US 220.
Contact: (919) 288-1776

Historical Museum
O. Henry and Dolly Madison are each the focus of an exhibit in the Greensboro Historical Museum with its period rooms, blacksmith house and transportation room.
Time: Museum: Tues.-Sat., 10 a.m.-5 p.m.; Sun., 2-5 p.m. House: Sat., 10 a.m.-5 p.m.; Sun., 2-5 p.m.
Place: 130 Summit Ave.
Contact: (919) 373-2043

Matisse Lithographs
The Weatherspoon Art Gallery is strong in contemporary art. The collection includes 75 Matisse lithographs and seven bronzes. Also well-represented

are 20th-century American artists.
Time: Tues.-Fri., 10 a.m.-5 p.m.; Sat.-Sun., 2-6 p.m. Closed during school breaks.
Place: McIver Bldg., University of North Carolina campus.
Contact: (919) 379-5770

Halifax
Historic Center
At the Historic Center, you'll learn about historic Halifax in an 18-minute film explaining the history of the Roanoke Valley. Fossils, a restored 1808 plantation home and a colonial cemetery (where you can make rubbings) are the other main attractions.
Time: Tues.-Sat., 9 a.m.-5 p.m.; Sun., 1-5 p.m.
Place: Halifax Center, St. David and Dobbs Sts.
Contact: (919) 583-7191

Hatteras Village
Atop a Lighthouse
There's a small visitor center and museum at Cape Hatteras Lighthouse, the tallest (208 feet) structure of its kind in the US. Although you can't go out on the balcony, you're allowed to climb to the top for

NORTH CAROLINA

Hatteras Village

a magnificent view of the coast.
Time: 9 a.m.-4:30 p.m.
Place: On NC 12, follow signs.
Contact: (919) 473-2111

Hickory

American Art

The Hickory Museum of Art features paintings of American artists from the 19th to the early 20th century, including American Impressionists and painters of the Hudson River school. In the European Gallery are works by Rousseau, Tintoretto and Turner.
Time: Mon.-Fri., 10 a.m.-5 p.m.; Sun., 3-5 p.m.
Place: Third St. and First Ave. NW.
Contact: (704) 327-8576

Kannapolis

Cotton to Cloth

In the visitor center at Cannon Mills you'll see a five-minute film showing the work of a loom in slow motion. Then take a one-hour walking tour of the grounds and plant to understand the transformation of cotton from 500-pound bales to finished cloth (you get a free washcloth as a sample).
Time: Visitor center: Mon.-Fri., 8:30 a.m.-4:30 p.m. Tours: Mon.-Fri., 9, 10:15 a.m. and 1 p.m.; please call ahead.
Place: West Ave.
Contact: (704) 933-1221, ext. 776
Note: No one under 16 admitted.

Kinston

Confederate Gunboat

The Caswell/Neuse Historic Site and Museum features a slide show on the Confederate gunboat CSS *Neuse*, sunk in 1865 and recovered in 1961 from Neuse River. You can see the boat outside. The Caswell Museum also offers a sound and light show on the first governor's life.
Time: Tues.-Sat., 9 a.m.-5 p.m.; Sun., 1-5 p.m.
Place: On Vernon Ave., 1 mi. W of town on US 70A.
Contact: (919) 522-2091

Kitty Hawk

12-Second Flight

It took only 12 seconds for the Wright brothers to etch their names in fame. It all happened in the grassed-over sand dunes of the Outer Banks in 1903. In

the visitor center at the Wright Brothers National Memorial is a replica of the first plane to take flight.
Time: June-Aug., 9 a.m-7 p.m; rest of year, 9 a.m-4:30 p.m.
Place: 2 mi. S of town on US Bypass 158.
Contact: (919) 473-2111

Kure Beach

Touch Pool

The North Carolina Marine Resources Center is an aquarium gallery. On the exhibit floor is a pool harboring sea creatures from urchins to horseshoe crabs, which you're encouraged to touch. Marine

life films are shown by advance request.
Time: June-Aug., Mon.-Fri., 9 a.m.-5 p.m.; Sat., 10 a.m.-5 p.m.; Sun., 1-5 p.m. Rest of year, Mon.-Fri., 9 a.m.-5 p.m.
Place: 1 mi. S of town on US 421.
Contact: (919) 458-8257

Fort Fisher

All that's left of Fort Fisher is a few mounds, but you can see a six-minute film recounting the "Fall of Fort Fisher," when the Federal Fleet bombarded the area with over two million pounds of projectiles.
Time: Tues.-Sat., 9 a.m.-5 p.m.; Sun., 1-5 p.m.
Place: 2 mi. S of town, off US 421.
Contact: (919) 458-5538

Laurinburg

Indian Museum

Devoted exclusively to the American Indian, this museum has a quarter of a million artifacts, including pipes, weapons, tools, canoes, baskets and homes—fine in its class.
Time: Tues.-Sun., 1-5 p.m.
Place: 607 Turnpike Rd.
Contact: (919) 276-5880

Linville Falls

Linville Gorge

Call for a free permit before hiking into this restricted wilderness area, known for its spectacular falls and lovely rhododendron-covered slopes rising above the Linville River. Paths have been cleared for hiking trails and climbing is excellent on rock formations such as The Chimneys, Hawk's Bill, Sitting Bear Rock and Table Rock.
Place: From Linville Falls, take US 221 to US 183.
Contact: (704) 652-4841
Note: Call no more than one month in advance for a free permit to enter this area. Do not enter without a permit, or you will be fined.

Manteo

National Seashore

Cape Hatteras National Seashore, 45 square miles of North Carolina's Outer Banks, is one of the finest and longest (70 miles) stretches of undeveloped seashore along the Atlantic Coast. Many of the islands are connected by free ferries, and access to beaches is also free. Nature walks, porpoises, and surf fishing are the area's main attractions.
Contact: Superintendent, Park Headquarters, Rt. 1, P. O. Box 675, Manteo, NC 27954; (919) 473-2117.

Mysterious Disappearance

At Fort Raleigh the first attempt to establish a colony took place in 1585. A second attempt ended with the mysterious disappearance of all settlers, explained in a short film. Little remains at the site.
Time: Visitor center: mid-June-Aug., Mon.-Sat., 8:30 a.m.-8:15 p.m., Sun., 8:30 a.m.-6 p.m.; call for hours during rest of year.
Place: 3 mi. N of town on US 64/264.
Contact: (919) 473-5772

Morgantown

UFOs?

Ever heard of the Brown Mountain Lights? These mysterious glowings have stumped scientists who must contend with reports of UFOs in the area. They have been talked about since the time of the Indians.
Time: Best on clear, moonless nights.
Place: Beacon Heights off Blue Ridge Pkwy., near Grandfather Mt. Or former site of Cold Springs Lodge on NC 181 or NC 105, near Marion.
Contact: (704) 437-3021

NORTH CAROLINA

Mount Gilead

Town Creek Indian Mound

In what was once a religious and political center for regional Indians, you'll find reconstructed Indian huts, an Indian mound and a museum with many artifacts of Indian life. There's a 15-minute slide show that you can see in the interpretive center.

Time: Tues.-Sat., 9 a.m.-5 p.m.; Sun., 1-5 p.m.
Place: 4 mi. E of town on NC 731.
Contact: (919) 439-6802

Mount Olive

Get in a Pickle

At Mount Olive Pickle Company you'll get to see the canning process and huge holding tanks where the brine is kept. You won't get in a pickle if you ask for a free sample.

Time: Mon.-Fri., 8:30 a.m.-noon and 1-4 p.m., by appt. only.
Place: 812 N. Chestnut St.
Contact: (919) 658-2535

Nags Head

Sand Dunes

So high are the sand dunes around Nags Head that they're used as the jumping-off point for hang-gliders. In fact, residents claim that Jockey Ridge (135 feet) may well be the highest dune along the East Coast! Beautiful view of the ocean and the sound.

Place: Just outside of town; ask locally for directions.
Contact: (919) 441-6093

New Bern

Ice Cream

Although there are no free samples at Maola Milk, there is a free tour where you'll see milk pasteurized and processed and ice cream made in the "mix" room.

Time: Tours: Mon., Tues., Thurs. and Fri., 9-11 a.m., by appt. only.
Place: 301 Ave. C.
Contact: (919) 638-1131

Ocracoke

Free Ferries

The state offers free automobile passage on ferries running between Hatteras and Ocracoke Islands. For information call the contact listed below.

Contact: (919) 928-4531

Pinehurst

Horse Training

During the winter and early spring months you can watch up to 400 horses being trained at the track on the edge of Pinehurst. Dozens of stables are located here, where you'll see jumpers, saddle horses, standard bred and harness horses.

Time: Oct.-May, Mon.-Sat., 7:30 a.m.-noon; best 9:30 a.m.
Place: .25 mi. E of town on US 5.
Contact: (919) 295-4371

Pineville

Polk Film

If you're interested in watching a 25-minute film on the life of James K. Polk, our 11th president, stop in at the Memorial State Historic Site in his honor.

Time: Tues.-Sat., 9 a.m.-5 p.m.; Sun., 1-5 p.m.
Place: On US 521.
Contact: (704) 889-7145

Raleigh

100,000 Artifacts

It would take weeks to see the thousands of artifacts owned by the North Carolina Museum of History. Some of the most enjoyable displays are a set of period costumes, period rooms and a model train layout.

Time: Tues.-Sat., 9 a.m.-5 p.m.; Sun., 1-6 p.m.
Place: 109 E. Jones St.
Contact: (919) 733-3894

Capitol Building

It took seven years to complete this classic building, restored to its original beauty in 1976. It rests in a six-acre park-like setting. Tours must be arranged through the visitor center.

Time: Mon.-Sat., 8:30 a.m.-5:30 p.m.; Sun., 1-6 p.m.
Place: Visitor center, 1301 N. Blount St. Capitol: Edenton St., Morgan St., Wilmington and Salisbury St.
Contact: (919) 733-3456

Exceptional Art

There's an historical sequence in the displays at the North Carolina Museum of Art, whose collection is now valued at over $8 million. Some of the dozens of masters represented here are Rembrandt, Rubens, Raphael and Renoir.

Time: Tues.-Sat., 10 a.m.-5 p.m.; Sun., 2-6 p.m.
Place: 107 E. Morgan St.
Contact: (919) 733-3248

Henry Clay Oak

"I'd rather be right than president" was the decision Henry Clay made while sitting under the limbs of this venerable oak. Henry was right—his famous "Texas Decision letter," written under this tree, cost him the election.

Place: In the yard of 407 N. Blount St.
Contact: (919) 733-3456

Live Snakes

In an area known for its abundant fauna and flora, you'd expect to find live snakes at the State Museum of Natural History. Indeed, you do, along with elk and buffalo mounts, Indian artifacts and a mineral collection.

Time: Mon.-Sat., 9 a.m.-5 p.m.; Sun., 1-6 p.m.
Place: 102 N. Salisbury St.
Contact: (919) 733-7450

Andrew Johnson's Birthplace

Although only open on a limited basis, you may want to stop and see Andrew Johnson's birthplace. Inside the Mordecai House are clothing and furnishings from five generations, as well as a portrait collection. Outside is an herb and flower garden typical of the early 1800s.

Time: June-Sept., Wed., 10 a.m.-noon; Sun., 2-4 p.m. Rest of year, Tues.-Thurs., 10 a.m.-1 p.m.
Place: 1 Mimosa St.
Contact: (919) 834-4844

Governor's Mansion

The convicts who completed this home in 1891 etched their

own initials in the handmade bricks. They can still be seen today on a tour arranged through the visitor center.

Time: Mansion: Oct.-Dec. and Feb.-May, by appt. only. Visitor center: Mon.-Sat., 8:30 a.m.-5:30 p.m.; Sun., 1-6 p.m.
Place: 301 N. Blount St.
Contact: (919) 733-3456

Free Tours

At the Capitol Area Visitors Center you can arrange for guided tours of the Legislative Building, Governor's Mansion, Capitol and other historic sites. Free brochures are given

NORTH CAROLINA

Raleigh

to anyone preferring to take self-guided tours.
Time: Mon.-Sat., 8:30 a.m.-5:30 p.m.; Sun., 1-6 p.m.
Place: 301 N. Blount St.
Contact: (919) 733-3456

Through a Glass Wall

A glass-walled observation gallery in the State Legislative Building allows you to watch the legislature in action. Only the legislative branch of the government can be found here, an arrangement that is unique in the country. You can pick up a brochure for a self-guided tour at the reception desk at the front of the building.
Time: Mon.-Fri., 8 a.m. - 5 p.m.; Sat., 9 a.m.-5 p.m.; Sun., 1-5 p.m.
Place: Jones St.
Contact: (919) 733-7928

Robbinsville

Water Slide

Slide down the slippery rocks in the streams flowing through Joyce Kilmer-Slickrock Wilderness Area. The water's chilly, just right on a sultry summer day.
Place: 1 mi. N of town on US 129; 13 mi. E on local road, clearly marked.
Contact: (704) 479-6431

Salisbury

Frito-Lay

On a tour of Frito-Lay you'll see the large vats where delicious Cheetos and Tostitos are made—and get free samples of these corn treats to boot!
Time: Tours: Tues. by appt. Office: Mon.-Fri., 8:30 a.m.-5 p.m.
Place: 900 N. Long St.
Contact: (704) 633-8100

Period Furnishings

The Rowan Museum is housed in the Maxwell Chambers House (1819) and is well-known for its period rooms. Outside is a sweet-smelling English garden with beautiful boxwood and wisteria.
Time: June-Sept., Tues.-Sun., 2-5 p.m.; rest of year, Thurs.-Sun., 2-5 p.m.
Place: 116 S. Jackson St.
Contact: (704) 633-5946

Saluda

Coon-Dog Barking Contest

In this contest judges award prizes for beauty and barking. Hounds hit their high wails at the base of a coon-topped tree.

The entire town of 600 turns out for the occasion!
Time: 1st Sat. after July 4th.
Place: Main St.
Contact: (704) 894-8236

Seagrove

Pottery Collection

Some of the pottery in the Potter's Museum was made in 1760. Exhibits are arranged in chronological sequence, up to the 1950s.
Time: Mon.-Sat., 10 a.m.-4 p.m.
Place: 1 mi. N of town on US 220.
Contact: (919) 873-7406

Spivey's Corner

National Hollerin' Contest

The tiny town of Spivey's Corner swells from a population of 49 to 12,049 during the National Hollerin' Contest. Held on the football field of Midway High School, the contest features the art of long, melodious calls once used by farmers to communicate in the hills of North Carolina.
Time: 3rd Sat. in June.
Place: Midway High School, on US 421.
Contact: Ermin Godwin, P.O. Box 332, Spivey's Corner, NC 28334; (919) 892-4133.

Weaverville

Pioneer Homestead

The Vance Pioneer Homestead includes a reconstructed log house, built in 1795, and farm buildings. On the third Sundays of April and September there's a "Pioneer Living Day" with churning, quilting and similar activities done by costumed participants.

Time: Tues.-Sat., 9 a.m.-5 p.m.; Sun., 1-5 p.m.
Place: 5 mi. E of town on Reems Creek Rd.
Contact: (704) 645-6706

Wilmington

See-Through Skeleton

In the New Hanover County Museum you'll find "Incredible You"—a see-through skeleton with body parts exposed—plus a doll collection, shells and photos of Wilmington.

Time: Tues.-Sat., 9 a.m.-5 p.m.; Sun., 2-5 p.m.
Place: 814 Market St.
Contact: (919) 763-0852

Spanish Moss and More

Moss-draped cypresses fringe a five-fingered lake bordered by Greenfield Gardens, noted for azaleas in full bloom in April.

Good spot for a picnic with a play area and petting zoo for the kids.

Time: Best Feb.-Apr.
Place: Entrance on Fourth St.
Contact: (919) 763-9871

Wilson

Tobacco Tour

You're in Tobacco Country! If you'd like to see warehouses and auctions in progress contact the local Chamber of Commerce, which will set up a tour for you. Tours begin with a 20-minute slide show that presents helpful background information.

Time: Mid-Aug.-early Nov., Mon.-Thurs., 9 a.m.

Place: 220 Broad St.
Contact: (919) 237-0165

Winston-Salem

Moravian Settlement

Carved from the wilderness in 1753, historic Bethabara includes the Gemein Haus, one of America's most beautiful examples of Moravian architecture. Costumed guides give tours of the settlement, and nature trails lead to God's Acre (graveyard).

Time: Easter-Nov., Mon.-Fri., 9:30 a.m.-4:30 p.m.; Sat.-Sun., 1:30-4:30 p.m.
Place: 2147 Bethabara Rd.
Contact: (919) 924-8191

Beer Testing

Sample a free glass of beer or a cold soft drink in the Brown Bottle hospitality room after a 25-minute tour of the Joseph Schlitz Brewing Company. You'll view its intricate brewing process from start to finish.

Time: Mon.-Fri., 9 a.m.-4 p.m.
Place: US 52S.
Contact: (919) 788-6710

Cigarette Tours

This is the world's largest cigarette manufacturing plant. Exhibits depict all phases of the industry, from growing tobacco to curing and storing

NORTH CAROLINA

Winston-Salem

it. Tours take you onto the floor where you see modern machines making and packaging the product.
Time: Mon.-Fri., 8 a.m.-10 p.m.
Place: N on Cherry St. off I-40 and E on Reynolds Blvd.
Contact: (919) 777-3718

Snakes and Birds

The Nature Science Center has an outdoor aviary and an indoor collection of snakes—from pythons to rattlers. You may also see wounded birds of prey recuperating in the aviary. Free films are shown on most weekends.
Time: Center: Mon.-Sat., 9 a.m.-5 p.m.; Sun., 1-5 p.m. Films: Sat.-Sun., 3 p.m. (please call in advance).
Place: Museum Dr.
Contact: (919) 767-6730

Statewide

Land of Flowering Shrubs

Following are the dates when more popular flowers and shrubs bloom. Major blooming varies only by a few days to a week each year—naturally, plants bloom earliest at lowest elevations.

Plant	Peak
Catalpa Tree	May
Crab Apple	May
Dogwood	Apr.-May
Flame Azalea	May-June
Japanese Magnolia	June-July
Japonica	Apr.-May
Mountain Laurel (Kalmia)	Mid-May-June
Magnolia	June-July
Mimosa	June
Royal Paulownia	Late Apr.-May
Primrose	June-Sept.
Queen Anne's Lace	June/ early Sept.
Rhododendron (many varieties)	Late Apr.-July
Sweet Shrub	May-early July
Trailing Arbutus	Mar.-early May
Trillium	Apr.-June
Violets	Mar.-early May
Wild Rose	June-July
Wisteria	May

Fall Color

With 223 mountains that rise 5,000 feet or higher in western North Carolina, you'll find trees turning color earlier in the chill fall air. Peak coloration in higher altitudes generally occurs in the third week of October. Recommended areas are Great Smoky Mountains National Park, Linville Gorge, Joyce Kilmer National Forest, Snowbird Mountains, and the counties of Yancey and Madison (follow the back roads).

Surf Casting

You don't need a license to fish in salt water along the lovely North Carolina shoreline. Surf fishing is excellent, especially at Avon, Buxton, Salvo and Waves along the Outer Banks.
Contact: (919) 733-4984

OKLAHOMA

ATTRACTIONS·THE BEST FREE
THE BEST FREE ATTRACTIONS·
FREE ATTRACTIONS·THE BEST
THE BEST F
FREE ATTR
ATTRACTIO
THE BEST F
ATTRACTIONS·
THE BEST FREE ATTRA
FREE ATTRACTIONS·THE BEST
ATTRACTIONS·THE BEST FREE
THE BEST FREE ATTRACTIONS·

- Bartlesville
- Tulsa
- ★ OKLAHOMA CITY
- Lawton

OKLAHOMA

Aline

Sod House

A two-room sod house of an early Oklahoma pioneer still stands here and is now a state-owned museum. By sod-house standards, it's a mansion: its floor is wood and its walls are plastered with gypsum mined at a nearby flood plain. There is also farm machinery, a blacksmith shop and two interpretive displays.

Time: Tues.-Fri., 9 a.m.-5 p.m.; Sat.-Sun., 2-5 p.m.
Place: 3 mi. SE of town on OK 8.
Contact: (405) 463-2441

Anadarko

Indian Exposition

This week-long celebration includes Indian dancers, horse-back riders, floats, and horse-back and greyhound racing.

Time: 2nd week in August; schedule varies year to year.
Place: E edge of town.
Contact: (405) 247-6651

Indian Museum

Historical and contemporary costumes of the Arapaho, Commanche, Caddo, Kiowa and Apache tribes are on display at the Southern Plains Indian Museum and Crafts Center. Other exhibits describe the peyote cult of the Southwest and the religious Ghost Dance of Western tribes.

Time: June 1-Sept. 30, Mon.-Sat., 9 a.m.-5 p.m.; Sun., 1-5 p.m. Oct. 1-May, Tues.-Sat., 9 a.m.-5 p.m.
Place: E edge of town on US 62.
Contact: (405) 247-6221

Ardmore

250-Year Old Dolls

More than 300 dolls, including a Queen Anne doll dating to 1728, are on display at the Eliza Cruce Hall Doll Museum. The dolls are from all over the world and are made of a variety of materials, including porcelain, wax, wood, china, plastic and leather.

Time: Mon.-Thurs., 10 a.m.-8:30 p.m.; Fri.-Sat., 10 a.m.-4 p.m.
Place: Public Library at Grand and E St. NW.
Contact: (405) 223-8290

Western Paintings

Russell and Remington are among the artists whose paintings are shown in the Charles B. Goddard Center for Visual and Performing Arts. The paintings date from the 19th century to the present. Many are rotated monthly, though some are part of the permanent collection.

Time: Mon.-Fri., 9:30 a.m.-4 p.m.; Sat., 11 a.m.-4 p.m.

Place: First Ave. and D St. SW.
Contact: (405) 226-0909

Bartlesville

Oil Magnate's Home

Tour the home of Frank A. Phillips, an early Oklahoma oil baron. The four-story house, furnished with Philippine mahogany, padded silk brocade walls, Irish crystal chandeliers and marble baths, is on the National Register of Historic Sites.

Time: Tues.-Fri., 9 a.m.-5 p.m.; Sat. and Sun., 2-5 p.m. (last tours begin at 4:30 p.m.).
Place: 1107 S. Cherokee Ave.
Contact: (918) 336-2491

Shrunken Heads

The exhibits at Woolaroc Museum include a display of shrunken heads. The heads of the hapless victims, now smaller than grapefruits, once belonged to South American Indians but were collected and brought to the United States in the 1930s. Other exhibits at the museum are from the Southwest—stone tools and clay pottery, Russell paintings, Navajo blankets and mounted animals.

Time: Apr. 1-Oct. 31, 10 a.m.-5 p.m.; Nov. 1-Apr. 1, 10 a.m.-5 p.m.

Place: 14 mi. SW of Bartlesville on US 123.
Contact: (918) 336-6747

Beaver

Cow Chip Toss

If you always suspected that politicians were adept at slinging mud and manure, this is your chance to confirm your suspicions. Every year the denizens of Beaver and outsiders get together to throw the stuff for distance and accuracy. Politicians have their own VIP division. Winners get trophies that look like—you guessed it

—cow chips. The record toss is charted at more than 176 feet.
Time: Sat. closest to Apr. 22 (Oklahoma Day). Schedule varies year to year.
Place: Fairgrounds on US 270 at the S edge of town.
Contact: (405) 625-4726

Broken Arrow

Rooster Day Celebration

Three days with a carnival, arts and crafts shows, a parade and a beauty pageant are scheduled each May—usually the weekend after Mother's Day—in downtown Broken Arrow. Witness the historic crowning of "Miss Chick."
Time: Schedule varies year to year.
Contact: (918) 251-1518

Cache

Wildlife

If you visit the Wichita Mountains National Wildlife Refuge, expect to see buffalo and Texas longhorn cattle—they may even stop your car as they cross the road. There is also a half-acre prairie dog town. A road leads up Mt. Scott, which

overlooks the entire refuge. Camping is free.
Place: 12 mi. N of town on OK 115.
Contact: (405) 429-3221

Cherokee

Salt Flats and Wildlife

You can climb a 20-foot tower in Salt Plains National Wildlife Refuge and view 28 square miles of salt flats, though mirages sometimes obscure the view. Or dig for salt crystals—some are six inches long. A mile-long nature trail winds through the refuge, which is home to songbirds, wild turkey, pheasant, quail and white-tailed deer. Camping at primitive sites is free.
Time: Dawn-dusk.
Place: OK 38, 15 mi. E of town.
Contact: (405) 626-4794

Cheyenne

Washita Battle Recounted

Battlefield relics and Indian artifacts are used in the Black Kettle museum to recreate the setting of the Battle of the Washita, Gen. George A. Custer's 1867 attack on the peaceful Washita encampment of

OKLAHOMA

Cheyenne

Chief Black Kettle. The actual battle site, now cultivated fields, is nearby and is marked with a memorial.
Time: Standard time, Mon.-Sat., 9 a.m.-5 p.m.; Sun., 1-5 p.m. Daylight-saving time, Mon.-Sat., 9 a.m.-7 p.m.; Sun., 1-7 p.m.
Place: US 283 and OK 47.
Contact: (405) 497-3929

Claremore

20,000 Guns

About 20,000 guns and accessories along with swords, knives and World War I posters and other military artifacts are packed into the J. M. Davis Gun Museum, a building that occupies an entire square block.
Time: Mon.-Sat., 8:30 a.m.-5 p.m.; Sun., 1-5 p.m.
Place: 333 N. Lynn Riggs Blvd.
Contact: (918) 341-5707

Will Rogers Memorial

Personal artifacts and two statues help describe the character of one of America's favorite humorists and best-known cowboys—Will Rogers. One room in this memorial building is a replica of Rogers' Santa Monica home. Several films are offered, including *Ropin' Fool*, which shows Rogers doing his rope tricks. Outside in a garden is the tomb of Rogers, his wife and his son.
Time: 8 a.m.-5 p.m.
Place: 1 mi. W of town on OK 88.
Contact: (918) 341-0719

Clinton

Artifacts

Stone arrowheads, scrapers, pipes and the bones of a mammoth that was uncovered near Foss Reservoir are part of the exhibits at the Western Trails Museum. There are also examples of early office and farm equipment, including a primitive x-ray machine and old printing machinery.
Time: Standard time, Mon.-Sat., 9 a.m.-5 p.m.; Sun., 1-5 p.m. Daylight-saving time, Mon.-Sat., 9 a.m.-7 p.m.; Sun., 1-7 p.m.
Place: SW edge of town at exit 65 from I-40.
Contact: (405) 323-1020

Dewey

Tom Mix Museum

The Lone Ranger's silver bullets are nothing compared to Tom Mix's equipment: a $15,000 saddle adorned with silver, as well as silver bits, bridles and belts. These and other possessions of the legendary silent film cowboy are on display. You also get to see some of his movies.
Time: Tues.-Fri., 9 a.m.-5 p.m.; Sat., 1-5 p.m.; Sun., 2-5 p.m.
Place: 721 N. Delaware St.
Contact: (918) 534-1555

Durant

Go to Jail

The activities at Durant Western Days are free—unless you are thrown in jail for not having a beard or costume. Bail is about 50 cents. There are turtle races and banana-eating contests for children and Frisbee-throwing contests for adults and kids.
Time: 3 days in mid- or late June. Schedule varies.
Place: Main St.
Contact: (405) 924-0848

El Reno

Pow-Wow

Four days of Indian ceremonial dancing, traditional dance contests and an arts and crafts show are scheduled every year in El Reno.
Time: Late June. Schedule varies year to year.
Place: W edge of town on Country Club Rd.
Contact: (405) 262-4822

Erick

50,000 Bees

The Wilhelm Honey Farm is one of the few places where you can closely watch some 50,000 honey bees at work without having to worry about getting stung. The insects, including the egg-laying queen bee, are working in a hive enclosed by a glass wall. Spring and summer are the best seasons to visit because that's when the bees are most active. The farm also boasts a candle factory (you can smell honey in beeswax).
Time: Mon.-Sat., 8 a.m.-6 p.m.
Place: On Honey Farm Rd., .25 mi. N of I-40 and 2 mi. W of OK 30.
Contact: (405) 526-3675

Fort Gibson

Stockade

About three dozen stone buildings, some log buildings and a reconstructed log stockade mark the site of old Fort Gibson, at one time the westernmost US outpost. Zachary Taylor, Robert E. Lee and other famous Americans served at this fort, built in 1824.
Time: Daylight-saving time, Mon.-Sat., 9 a.m.-7 p.m.; Sun., 9 a.m.-1 p.m. Standard time, 9 a.m.-5 p.m.

Place: .5 mi. N of town on OK 80, 10 mi. E of Muskogee.
Contact: (918) 478-2669

Goodwell

Bandits and Arrowheads

"No man's land" described the Oklahoma panhandle during territorial days—a strip of unregulated land that was a haven for outlaws. Its history is told in No Man's Land Museum on the Panhandle State University campus. One of the most popular exhibits is a collection of arrowheads, which includes stone points 10,000 years old and steel points fashioned in the 1800s.
Time: Tues.-Fri., 9 a.m.-noon, 1-5 p.m.; Sat.-Sun., 1-5 p.m.
Place: US 54 in town.
Contact: (405) 349-2670

Grove

Pioneer Village

About 50 buildings, including a church, school house, bank and doctor's office, dot Har-Ber Village, a recreation of an early-day frontier town. Dishes, dollhouses, stuffed animals and minerals also are on display.
Time: May 1-Oct. 31, 9 a.m.-6 p.m.; closed Nov.-Apr.

Place: 3.3 mi. W of town on Lake Rd.
Contact: (918) 786-5882

Guthrie

Biggest Masonic Building

The three-storey Scottish Rite Temple, a Doric building constructed in 1923, is one of the largest buildings in the world used exclusively for Masonic activities. Each room has a different decor.
Time: Mon.-Thur., 7:30 a.m.-noon, 1-5:30 p.m.
Place: 900 E. Oklahoma St.
Contact: (405) 282-1281

Territorial Museum

A complete frontier wood-frame house, built during the land rush of 1889, sits amidst the other exhibits in the Oklahoma Territorial Museum. The museum is a new building attached to the 79-year old Carnegie Library, which was the site of the inaugurations of the last territorial governor and the first state governor.
Time: Tues.-Fri., 9 a.m.-5 p.m.; Sat.-Sun., 2-5 p.m.
Place: 402 E. Oklahoma Ave.
Contact: (405) 282-1889

Hartshorne

Blue Mountain Festival

Watch a parade, dance to blue-grass music, listen to gospel music and take in a free bar-b-que. Watermelon, by the way, is free at this week-long festival.

Time: The dates of the festival vary, but always include July 4.

Contact: (918) 297-2683

Heavener

Conser Mansion

A two-story, five-bedroom house built by Peter Conser in 1894 is open to tours. Conser was a leader of the Choctaw Lighthorsemen, a law enforcement group.

Time: Tues.-Fri., 9 a.m.-5 p.m.; Sat.-Sun., 2-5 p.m.

Place: 4 mi. S and 3.5 mi. W of town.

Contact: (918) 653-2493

Kingfisher

Chisholm Trail Museum

Kingfisher's first bank, a small wooden-frame building, is part of the Chisholm Trail Museum. There are also a log cabin, early farm machinery, a one-room school house and a collection of arrowheads. Nearby is the Seay Mansion, a spacious three-storey house furnished as it was in the 1890s.

Time: Standard time, Mon.-Sat., 9 a.m.-5 p.m.; Sun., 1-5 p.m. Daylight-saving time, Mon.-Sat., 9 a.m.-7 p.m.; Sun., 1-7 p.m.

Place: 605 Zellers Ave.

Contact: (405) 375-5176

Lawton

Big Gun Display

Artillery—from a small cannon of the early 1600s to a 280 mm cannon that fires a nuclear projectile—are the centerpieces of the military exhibits at the Fort Sill Military Reservation. Exhibits are in the original post buildings, some dating to 1869. A complete tour, which includes a 26-minute film, takes at least 3 1/2 hours.

Time: 9 a.m.-4:30 p.m.

Place: 4 mi. N of town on H. E. Bailey Turnpike.

Contact: (405) 351-4500

Great Plains History

Forty display cases at the Museum of the Great Plains reveal the area's history, from prehistoric times to the settlement of the state. Another display is the uprooted and transported train depot from Elgin, OK. A big steam locomotive sits nearby.

Time: Mon.-Fri., 8 a.m.-5 p.m.; Sat., 10 a.m.-5:30 p.m.; Sun., 1:30-5:30 p.m.

Place: 601 Ferris Blvd.

Contact: (405) 353-5675

Sunrise Pageant

More than 20,000 people gather on a hillside for the Witchita Mountains Easter Sunrise Service, an historical play representing the life of Christ. More than 500 locals act in the pageant, which has run for more than 50 years. People begin arriving early Saturday for the performance, which is in a natural rock amphitheater wired with lights and a sound system.

Time: Easter, 2 a.m.-sunrise.
Place: The Holy City in the Witchita Mountains National Wildlife Refuge on OK 49, 22 mi. NW of town.
Contact: (405) 429-3361

Lindsay

Rancher's Mansion

Imported cherry wood decorates the rooms of this sandstone mansion built by rancher-farmer Frank Murray in 1880. When built, it was one of the only homes and surely the only mansion for miles around. Murray, a Chickasaw Indian, owned 20,000 acres of the surrounding land.

Time: Tues.-Fri., 9 a.m.-5 p.m.; Sat.-Sun., 1-5 p.m.
Place: 2 mi. S of town on OK 76.
Contact: (405) 756-3826

Mangum

Rattlesnake Hunt

Go down to Mangum and round up some rattlesnakes at this yearly hunt. Not only can you watch or participate for free, you may win a prize for bringing in the biggest snake ($100) or the greatest combined weight of snakes ($150). Market prices are paid for the snakes, which are hauled off to the butcher's. There is a $1-a-pound bonus for bringing in your snakes on the first day of the round-up.

Time: 3 days in late Apr.; schedule varies year to year.
Contact: (405) 782-2444

Marietta

Frontier Celebration

A Western parade of horses, floats and bands winds past the Love County Courthouse in Marietta once a year to launch the two-day Love County Frontier Days Celebration. The second day of the event begins with breakfast on the courthouse lawn. There also are games for children, archery and beard contests and an art show.

Time: 1st weekend in June.
Place: Love County Courthouse.
Contact: (405) 276-3102

Muskogee

Historians' Home

The home of two of Oklahoma's outstanding historians, Grant and Carolyn Foreman, is open for tours. The single-storey, white, wood-frame house is filled with original furnishings and the Foremans' private historical and art collections.

Time: Tues.-Fri., 9 a.m.-5 p.m.; Sat.-Sun., 2-5 p.m.
Place: 1419 W. Okmulgee St.
Contact: (918) 682-0133

Norman

Mammoth Exhibits

The huge skeleton of a mammoth unearthed in Oklahoma dominates the fossil exhibit hall at the Stovall Museum of Science and History at the University of Oklahoma. Giant dinosaur bones and tiny prehistoric starfish also are there. Archaeological, Indian and natural history displays round out the exhibits.

Time: Mon.-Fri., 9 a.m.-5 p.m.; Sat.-Sun., 1-5 p.m.
Place: 1335 Asp Ave.
Contact: (405) 325-4711

US Painters

The Museum of Art at the University of Oklahoma features exhibits of mid-20th century American painters and artwork by Pueblo and Southern Plains Indians. It also displays European, Oriental and Oceanic art.

Time: Tues.-Fri., 10 a.m.-4 p.m.; Sat., 10 a.m.-1 p.m.; Sun., 1-4 p.m.
Place: 410 W. Boyd St.
Contact: (405) 325-3272

OKLAHOMA

Oklahoma City

Art Festivals

Two art festivals—a sizeable one in spring and a smaller one in autumn—are presented in Oklahoma City. The Spring Festival of the Arts, scheduled during the last full week in April, includes some 200 artists. The Fall Festival usually includes 40 to 50 artists and is held in September or October. In addition to the paintings, sculptures and other visual art, there is music of various kinds.

Time: Schedule varies year to year.
Place: In the spring: Civic Center Park, Walker Ave. and Couch Dr. In the fall: Kerr Park, Broadway and Robert S. Kerr Ave.
Contact: (405) 521-1426

Governor's Mansion

Tour the mansion that has been home to more than a dozen Oklahoma chief executives. The graystone 19-room Dutch Colonial mansion was built in 1928.

Time: Wed., 1-4 p.m.
Place: 820 N.E. 23rd St.
Contact: (405) 521-2342

Hitler's Belongings

A display of memorabilia collected from Hitler's apartments is one of the chief exhibits at the 45th Infantry Division Museum. Some of Bill Mauldin's original World War II "Willie and Joe" cartoons also are on display along with other military wares.

Time: Tues.-Fri., 9 a.m.-5 p.m.; Sat.-Sun., 1-5 p.m.
Place: 2145 N.E. 36th St.
Contact: (405) 424-5313

Oiling the Wheels of Government

An oil well on the grounds of the State Capitol pumps 16 barrels of black gold from underneath the capitol building each day. Inside the capitol, murals decorating the rotunda recount the history of the state.

Time: Mon.-Sat., 8 a.m.-4 p.m.
Place: N.E. 22nd and Lincoln Blvd.
Contact: (405) 521-3356

Oklahoma Historical Society

An extensive collection of Indian relics—pottery, paintings and weapons—are on display at the Historical Society. Other exhibits describe the state's history from the days of prehistoric creatures through the days of the Dust Bowl and the oil boom.

Time: Mon.-Sat., 9 a.m.-5 p.m.
Place: 2100 N. Lincoln Blvd.
Contact: (405) 521-2491

Oologah

Will Rogers's Birthplace

Visit Will Rogers's two-story wood-frame birthplace. The house of the famous humorist, decorated in period settings, was moved a few hundred yards from its original site when a nearby reservoir flooded.

Time: 8 a.m.-5 p.m.
Place: 1 mi. N of town on US 169 and then 2 mi. E.
Contact: (918) 341-0719

Pawhuska

Oldest Scout Troup

A monument in the Osage County Historical Museum commemorates the founding of America's first scout troop in this town in 1909. There also are military exhibits covering US wars from the Civil War to World War II.

Time: 9 a.m.-5 p.m.
Place: 700 N. Lynn Ave.
Contact: (918) 287-9924

Pawnee

Pawnee Bill

The early 20th-century home of local folk hero Pawnee Bill is on display and is filled with personal effects from his Pawnee Bill Wild West Show. Original furnishings complete the 14-room house. Outside is a buffalo and Texas longhorn pasture.

Time: Standard time, Mon.-Sat., 9 a.m.-5 p.m.; Sun., 1-5 p.m. Daylight-saving time, Mon.-Sat., 9 a.m.-7 p.m.; Sun., 1-7 p.m.
Place: 1 mi. W of town on US 64.
Contact: (918) 762-2513

Perry

Land Rush Festival

A parade, exhibits and entertainment during the Cherokee Strip Celebration commemorate the opening of this area to settlement. The four-day festival includes exhibits of livestock, agriculture and business.

Time: Mid-Sept.
Contact: (405) 336-4684

Pioneer Artifacts

Tools and other artifacts from Oklahoma settlement days are on display at the Cherokee Strip Museum and Henry S. Johnston Library. The library holds the books collected by Johnston, the governor from 1926-27.

Time: Tues.-Fri., 9 a.m.-5 p.m.; Sat.-Sun., 2-5 p.m.
Place: Fir Ave., .25 mi. E of I-35.
Contact: (405) 336-2405

Ponca City

Oilman's House

Tour the mansion of oilman E. W. Marland, the tenth governor of Oklahoma. The house, built in the early 1900s, has a hanging stairway, an indoor pool and period settings. One exhibit is the studio of sculptor Bryant Baker, who made the famous Pioneer Woman statue in Ponca City. Other exhibits include Indian artifacts.

Time: Mon., Wed.-Sat., 10 a.m.-5 p.m.; Sun., 1-5 p.m.
Place: 1000 E. Grand.
Contact: (405) 762-6123

Pioneer Woman Museum

The centerpiece of this museum is the statue by Bryant Baker that shows a pioneer woman striding forward clutching a Bible in one hand and her small son's hand in the other. Bryant's statue, dedicated in 1930, was proclaimed the winner in a contest to capture the spirit of pioneer women.

Time: Standard time, Mon.-Sat., 9 a.m.-5:30 p.m.; Sun., 1-5:30 p.m. Daylight-saving time, Mon.-Sat., 9 a.m.-7 p.m.; Sun., 1-7 p.m.
Place: 701 Monument Rd.
Contact: (405) 765-6108

Sallisaw

Sequoyah's Home

Tour the hewn-log cabin built in 1830 by Sequoyah, the inventor of the 84-character Cherokee alphabet.

Time: Tues.-Fri., 8 a.m.-5 p.m.; Sun., 2-5 p.m.
Place: 12 mi. NE of town on OK 101.
Contact: (918) 775-2413

Sapulpa

Frankoma Pottery

See the way pottery is formed and fired. The shop displays its

OKLAHOMA

Sapulpa

wares as table settings. Many of the pieces have typically Western or Indian designs.
Time: Mon.-Fri., 9-11:30 a.m., 1-2:30 p.m.
Place: 2 mi. N of town on Frankoma Rd.
Contact: (918) 224-5511

Shawnee

Egyptian Mummy

The diverse exhibits in the Mabee-Ferrer Collection of St. Gregory's Abbey and College include an Egyptian mummy, Southwest Indian art, more than 500 European and US paintings, 6,000 artifacts and many etchings, engravings and lithographs.
Time: Tues.-Sun., 1-4 p.m.
Place: 1900 W. McArthur Dr.
Contact: (405) 273-9870

Spiro

Indian Mounds

Nine Indian mounds, ranging in age from 500 to 1,000 years, are the centerpiece of Spiro Mounds State Park. Some mounds were for ceremony, others for burial and others for home foundations. The Craig Mound, the largest, is 300 feet long, 115 feet wide and 34 feet tall. An interpretive center houses grave relics.
Time: Mon.-Sat., 8 a.m.-5 p.m.; Sun., 1-5 p.m.
Place: 3.5 mi. E of town on OK 271, then 2 mi. N.
Contact: (918) 962-2062

Stilwell

Strawberry Festival

Get free strawberries and ice cream at this festival, held in Oklahoma's prime strawberry region. The event also includes a parade, a berry contest and a queen contest.
Time: 2nd Sat. in May.
Contact: (918) 774-7143

Stroud

Throw a Brick

Every year, residents of Stroud gather to throw bricks and rolling pins. The strange rite is part of an international competition of Stroudians in four countries. The records of the best efforts from Stroud, OK, are compared to results from residents of the towns of Stroud in England, Australia and Canada. The Oklahoma town supplies the bricks for practice and competition.
Time: July 4 for preliminaries; 3rd Sat. in July for international finals.

Place: Foster Park on NE edge of town.
Contact: (918) 968-3321

Sulphur

Sulphur Springs

Sulphur springs, discovered long ago by the Chickasaw Indians, can be seen in the Chickasaw National Recreation Area. The sulphur, freshwater and bromide springs have been used for medicinal purposes (though their water should be drunk only on the advice of a physician). A small herd of buffalo roams part of the area. A nature center is open during the day.
Place: Main intersection in town.
Contact: (405) 622-3161

Tahlequah

Cherokee Pow-Wow

Ceremonial dances, archery contests and other activities can be seen during the three-day Cherokee National Holiday at the Cherokee Arts and Crafts Center. Paintings, baskets, pottery and other items are on display in the center.
Time: Labor Day weekend.
Place: 3 mi. S of town on US 62.
Contact: (918) 456-6031

Murrell Home

This mansion, built by George Murrell in about 1845, was a center of social activity in antebellum days. Though looted during the Civil War, it was one of the few homes in the area to escape destruction. The home and a nearby nature trail are accessible to the handicapped.

Time: Standard time, Mon.-Sat., 9 a.m.-5 p.m.; Sun., 1-5 p.m. Daylight-saving time, Mon.-Sat. 9 a.m.-7 p.m.; Sun., 1-7 p.m.
Place: 3 mi. S of town on US 82, then 1 mi. E.
Contact: (918) 456-2751

Talihina

Scenic Drive

The beautiful autumn drive through the Winding Stair Mountains of Ouachita National Forest begins in Talihina, OK, and leads eastward for 50 miles to Mena, AR. From the highlands, the surrounding country sometimes is enveloped in a dreamy haze.

Time: Most colorful in fall.
Place: Route begins 7 mi. NE of Talihina on US 271.
Contact: (918) 647-9178

Tulsa

Rows and Rows of Roses

More than 9,000 rose bushes of 250 varieties decorate the 4½ acres of the Municipal Rose Garden, which is part of 40-acre Woodward Park.

Time: Anytime, though peak blooms are in mid-May and mid-October.
Place: Peoria and 23rd Sts.
Contact: (918) 747-2709

Bread Factory

Smell that heady aroma of baking bread as you tour the Rainbow Baking Co. Learn how the dough is mixed and baked; then see how the bread is cooled and wrapped, ready to send off to stores. Watch the employees as they produce white and whole-wheat bread and buns.

Time: Wed., noon-4 p.m.
Place: 1650 E. 11th St.
Contact: (918) 587-4181

Contemporary Art

The Alexandre Hogue Gallery of Art features changing month-long displays of contemporary art. Recent exhibits include California citrus labels and works by high school students and visiting local artists.

Time: During school year only, Mon.-Fri., 8 a.m.-noon, 1-5 p.m.; Sun., 2-5 p.m.
Place: Phillips Hall, Tulsa University campus, 600 S. College Ave.
Contact: (918) 592-6000

International Mayfest

Singers, dancers, a senior citizen's band, puppeteers, magicians and jugglers roam the streets and sidewalks of the downtown mall on Main St. during the International Mayfest. There also are arts and crafts booths.

Time: Mid-May. Schedule varies year to year.
Place: 6 blocks along Main St.
Contact: (918) 583-5794

Jewish Art

The Rebecca and Gershon Fenster Gallery of Jewish Art claims to have the third largest collection of its sort in the US. The exhibits, some nearly 7,000 years old, were collected from Poland, Spain, Russia, India, Iran, Germany and Morocco.

Time: Mon.-Sat., 1-4 p.m.; Sun., 2-4 p.m. By appt. only (phone ahead).
Place: 1719 S. Owasso Ave.
Contact: (918) 583-7121

North American Zoo

The Tulsa Zoological Park includes a North American "living museum" with animals such as polar and black bears,

OKLAHOMA

Tulsa

buffalo, peccary, arctic and kit foxes and bobcats. There also are displays of fresh- and salt-water fish, as well as more typical zoo animals on the 68-acre site—lions, tigers, apes and others. The zoo is part of 2,820-acre Tulsa Park, which is owned by the city.

Time: Free entry on Mon. and Sat. as follows: Apr.-Aug., 10 a.m.-6:30 p.m.; Sept.-Nov., 10 a.m.-5:30 p.m.; Dec.-Mar., 10 a.m.-4:30 p.m.
Place: 5701 E. 36th St. N.
Contact: (918) 835-8471
Note: Fees charged on other days.

Octoberfest

The sound of German polka bands fills the air during Octoberfest in Tulsa. There are also folk singers and the Tulsa International Dancers.

Time: 3rd weekend in Oct., Fri.-Sun.
Place: River Park on W bank of Arkansas River between 11th St. and 21st St.
Contact: (918) 582-0051

Oil Refinery

Tour the large Sun Oil Co. Tulsa Refinery and learn how a big oil firm refines oil and tries to control air and water pollution at the same time.

Time: Mon.-Fri., 10 a.m. and 2 p.m.; Sat., 10 a.m.
Place: 1700 S. Union Ave.
Contact: (918) 586-7601

Oral Roberts University

Climb a 200-foot-tall glass and steel prayer tower, tour a six-story hexagonal library and view other architectural attractions at this famous institution for evangelical teaching.

Time: Mon.-Sat., 9 a.m.-5 p.m.; Sun., 1-5 p.m.
Place: 81st and S. Lewis Ave.
Contact: (918) 492-6161

Raft Race

Watch rafts race a 9.3-mile stretch of the Arkansas river. There are divisions for rubber kayaks and inflatable crafts, both commercial and home-made.

Time: Labor Day, 9 a.m.-dark.
Place: Race starts at River City Park in Sand Springs, 7 mi. W of town on US 64; it ends at 31st St. and Riverside Dr.
Contact: (918) 582-0051

Western Artists

Works by Remington, Russell, Audubon and many other American artists are on display at the Thomas Gilcrease Institute of American History and Art. Many exhibits trace the development of art in the New World.

Time: Mon.-Sat., 9 a.m.-5 p.m.; Sun., 1-5 p.m.
Place: 1400 N. 25th W. Ave.
Contact: (918) 581-5311

Watonga

Historic Home

Tour the home of T. B. Ferguson, Oklahoma's sixth territorial governor. The three-storey wood-frame house is topped by a cupola and surrounded by a white picket fence. It was built in 1901. In its back lot sits the first city jail, built in 1893.

Time: Standard time, Mon.-Sat., 9 a.m.-5 p.m.; Sun., 1-5 p.m. Daylight-saving time, Mon.-

Sat., 9 a.m.-7 p.m.; Sun., 1-7 p.m.
Place: 519 N. Weigel.
Contact: (405) 623-5069

Waurika

Cattle Drives

The challenges of driving cattle over hundreds of miles in the arid West are recreated at the Chisholm Trail Historical Museum. The exhibits, which include weapons, saddles and other artifacts of the pioneers and cattlemen, trace the history of the Chisholm Trail.
Time: Tues.-Fri., 9 a.m.-5 p.m.; Sat.-Sun., 2-5 p.m.
Place: US 81 and US 70.
Contact: (405) 228-2166

Waynoka

Hunt Rattlesnakes

Eat your fill at a free bean feed in the morning and then begin searching the cliffs and gullies around town to find rattlesnakes. Prizes are given to the most successful hunters, and the reptiles are sold at market prices to the local butcher. If you plan to join the hunt, wear heavy boots and carry a gunnysack and long, forked stick.
Time: 1st weekend after Easter.
Place: Waynoka City Hall.
Contact: (405) 824-5911

Dune Buggy Haven

The shifting sand dunes near Waynoka have been set aside especially for people with off-road vehicles. The dunes, which range in height from 20 to 70 feet, change with the wind patterns and usually peak (literally) with the stiff breezes of early spring or late summer. To drive over them, you need a dune buggy, a four-wheel-drive vehicle or a similar jalopy. Camping (without electrical hookups) in the 1,480-acre Little Sahara State Recreation Area is free, though a fee is charged for entry during the summer.
Time: No entry fee Oct. 1-Apr. 30.
Place: 4 mi. S of town on US 281.
Contact: (405) 824-1471

Wewoka

Seminole Nation Museum

Exhibits trace the forced migration of the Seminoles from their native Florida along the Trail of Tears to Oklahoma. Seminole homes and activities are portrayed and Seminole artifacts displayed.
Time: Daily, 1-5 p.m.
Place: 524 S. Wewoka.
Contact: (405) 257-5580

Statewide

Free Coffee

You'll find free coffee—as well as restrooms and picnic facilities—at many of Oklahoma's Visitor Information Centers.
Time: Daily, 8:30 a.m.-noon.
Place: 10 mi. S of the Oklahoma-Kansas border on I-35.
In Enid at intersection of US 60/64, US 81 and OK 15.
14 mi. W of Oklahoma-Arkansas border on I-40.
2 mi. N of Oklahoma-Texas border on US 69/75.
1 mi. N of Oklahoma-Texas border on I-35.
US 277 at Gore Ave. exit in Lawton.
9 mi. E of Oklahoma-Texas border on I-40.
Contact: (405) 521-2406

State Parks

Entry to and camping in Oklahoma's 31 state parks is free. So are many other park activities. In many cases, only the electrical hookups for campers and recreational vehicles cost money. For more information, call the Oklahoma Tourism and Recreation Department.
Contact: In Oklahoma, (800) 522-8565; in Oklahoma City or out of state, (405) 521-2464.

OKLAHOMA

Trail Maps

There is a multitude of trails in Oklahoma state parks, all of which are free to enter. A map from the Oklahoma Tourism and Recreation Department shows most of these trails for hiking, horseback riding and a variety of other outdoor activities.

Contact: Oklahoma Tourism and Recreation Dept., 500 Will Rogers Bldg., Oklahoma City, OK 73105; (405) 521-2409.

SOUTH CAROLINA

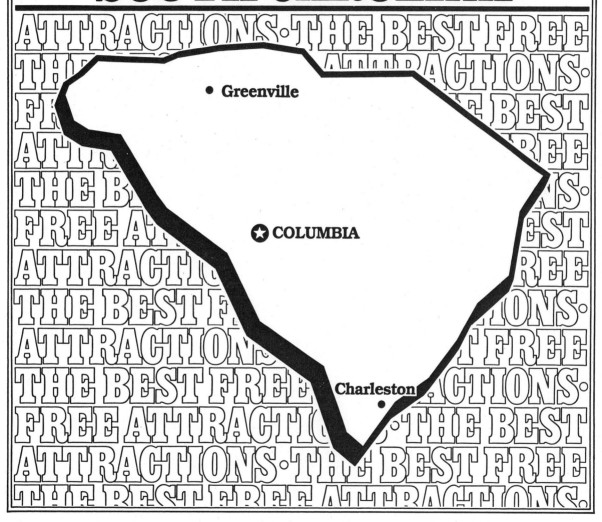

ATTRACTIONS·THE BEST FREE THE ATTRACTIONS· FREE THE BEST ATTR FREE THE BE FREE A ATTRACTI THE BEST F ATTRACTI THE BEST FR FREE ATTRACTI ATTRACTIONS·THE BEST FREE THE BEST FREE ATTRACTIONS·

- Greenville

☆ COLUMBIA

Charleston

SOUTH CAROLINA

Aiken

Thoroughbred Racing Hall of Fame

During the off-season from November to March, Aiken is a horse town with the Triple Crown (admission charged) drawing 10,000 people in the third week in March. However, the Hall of Fame and surrounding Hopeland Gardens, with their moss-covered spreading oaks, are open free of charge. Champions are enshrined in the Hall, which was vastly improved by a 1980 grant. Concerts, theater performances and children's programs are also free. And at sunup you can see horses worth $100,000 training nearby.

Time: Gardens: daylight hours. Hall of Fame, Tues.-Sun., 2-5 p.m. Concerts: Mon., 7 p.m. Theater: Thurs., 7 p.m. Children's programs: Sat., 2-3 p.m.
Place: Off Whiskey Rd. at 149 Dupree Pl.
Contact: (803) 649-7700

Beaufort

Hunting Island State Park

One of the most popular state parks attracts over a million visitors each year. Noted for its semi-tropical beauty and abundant deer, raccoon, and waterfowl. Swimming and surf casting from a wide, smooth beach. Climb all 181 steps of the spiral staircase leading to the top of a 140-foot lighthouse for a breathtaking view of the island, ocean, and marshes.

Place: 16 mi. SE of town on US 21.
Contact: (803) 838-2011

Photogenic Port

Some houses in the picturesque port of Beaufort date back to the early 1700s. Park the car and take a walk to get a feeling of this old town's charm.

Charleston

Dock Street Theater

Not the first theater in the US, but the site of the first theater, which burned down to be replaced by the Planters Hotel. The hotel was later reconverted to a theater by changing the courtyard to a stage area and some of the bedrooms to a balcony. Small and very intimate (500 seats), it can be visited free of charge, although there is a fee for performances.

Time: Mon.-Fri., 10 a.m.-5 p.m.
Place: 135 Church St., at crossing with Queen St.
Contact: (803) 722-7521

Fort Moultrie

The fort was used as a seacoast fortification for 171 years, from 1776 to 1947. A tour of the grounds is like entering a time capsule. Each period of the bastion is brought to life through detailed restoration. Both recreated Civil and Revolutionary War encampments include dress of the period. There's a 20-minute film too.

Time: Mid-Mar.-mid-Oct., 9 a.m.-6 p.m.; rest of year, 8:30 a.m.-5 p.m. Film starts on the hour.
Place: 1214 W. Middle St. on Sullivan's Island.
Contact: (803) 883-3123

Full Dress Military Parades

At The Citadel, which calls itself the "West Point of the South," you can see full-dress parades each Friday afternoon and visit the museum as well. The museum outlines the school's history and has Civil War displays.

Time: Dress parades: 3:45 p.m. each Fri., weather permitting. Museum: Mon.-Fri., 2-5 p.m.; Sat., 9 a.m.-5 p.m.; Sun., 10 a.m.-5 p.m.
Place: Citadel campus.
Contact: Museum: (803) 792-6846; parades: (803) 792-5006

Historic Walking Tour

The History Trail is marked with signs in the older part of the city, and it is visited by thousands of people yearly for its historic homes and churches. Outstanding churches include St. Michael's and St. Philips; the Huguenot Church now tends to be closed despite its historical significance. The "Historic Charleston" brochure is available free from most hotels, the Chamber of Commerce and businesses oriented to tourists.

Contact: Visitor Information Center, 85 Calhoun St., P.O. Box 975, Charleston, SC 29402; (803) 722-8338.

Hunley Museum

The Confederate States devised the first submarine, *H. L. Hunley,* in 1863. It sunk twice in training sessions, killing both crews. Finally, it was used to ram a torpedo into the Federal sloop-of-war *Housatonic,* which sank but took the Hunley with it. The 25-foot long, 4-foot wide replica rests outside the museum, which houses Civil War naval displays and artifacts.

Time: 10 a.m.-5 p.m.
Place: 50 Broad St., at Church St.
Contact: (803) 723-7983

Navy Ship Tour

At the Charleston Naval Base, you can board a surface ship, such as a frigate or destroyer, on a fully guided tour. It is not a comprehensive program, but a great hit with most kids!

Time: Weekends and major holidays only, 1-4 p.m.
Place: Charleston Naval Base, on Viaduct Rd. off Spruill Ave. Well-marked from I-26.
Contact: (803) 743-3940
Note: Photos permitted on ship only.

Spoleto

Billed as the "world's most comprehensive festival of the arts," Spoleto offers everything from craft fairs and twilight poetry to organ recitals and chamber music. All performances are free except for the After Hours Jazz and Fringe Theatre Series.

Time: Late May and early June.
Contact: Call toll-free (800) 845-7108 outside state. Inside SC call (803) 723-7641.

Chattooga River

National Wild and Scenic River

Beginning on the crest of the Blue Ridge Mountains in

North Carolina, the sparkling Chattooga River divides South Carolina and Georgia for more than 40 miles and is familiar to millions as the location for the filming of *Deliverance.* The river drops an average of 49.3 feet per mile, sometimes following a narrow and treacherous route over rapids, around boulders and through rock flumes. A national forest flanks the river for primitive camping and hiking trails.

Place: 13 mi. W of Westminster on SC 76.
Contact: (803) 647-5336

SOUTH CAROLINA

Cherokee Hills

Cherokee Foothills Scenic Highway

Instead of driving through South Carolina on I-85, try this scenic route extending from I-85 near the North Carolina border in a 130-mile crescent to I-85 at the Georgia line. In the spring blooming dogwood and mountain laurel make it a feast for the eyes (and the nose).

Place: Head NW off I-85 at Gaffney on SC 11. Follow it for 130 mi. to reconnect with I-85 W of Anderson. Pass Pleasant Ridge, Caesars Head and Keowee Toxaway State Parks en route.

Clemson

Fort Hill Mansion

Built in 1803 and once the home of John C. Calhoun (Confederate bank notes bore his image), this lovely antebellum mansion retains many of the original furnishings, including George Washington's sofa.

Time: Tues.-Sat., 10 a.m.-5:30 p.m. (closed for lunch); Sun., 2-6 p.m.
Contact: (803) 656-2475

Hanover House

The historic house, a classic example of Huguenot architecture, was built in 1760 and stood in the southern part of the state for more than 200 years, where it served both as a residence and a frontier fort. Threatened by plans to construct a dam in 1940, it was painstakingly dismantled, moved and restored on the east end of campus.

Time: Tues.-Sat., 10 a.m.-5:30 p.m. (closed for lunch); Sun., 2-6 p.m.
Place: On the Clemson University campus near the Agricultural Bldg.
Contact: (803) 656-2241

Columbia

America's First Passenger Train

A replica of America's first passenger train, the *Best Friend*, is on display at Sesquicentennial State Park, which has a swimming lake and picnic grounds for relaxation. Also you'll find a reassembled log house dating back to 1756 on the grounds.

Time: Year-round.
Place: 13 mi. NE of town on US 1.
Contact: (803) 788-2706

Confederate Relic Room and Museum

Artifacts and uniforms from the Revolutionary War and all wars since then, with a special emphasis on South Carolina history. Guns and sabres, flags and regimental banners, and even pictures of Southern heroes from the Confederate era.

Time: Mon.-Fri., 9 a.m.-5 p.m.; weekends by appt.
Place: In the War Memorial Bldg. at 920 Sumter St., on corner of Pendleton St.
Contact: (803) 758-2144

Governor's Mansion

Although built as an officers' quarters in 1855, it has served as the official residence for South Carolina's governors since 1868. Priceless antiques fill the public rooms and can be seen on brief tours. Arrange for them by calling ahead.

Time: Tues.-Thurs., by appt. only.
Place: 800 Richland St.
Contact: (803) 758-3452

McKissick Museums

A series of museums in one building at the head of the Horseshoe on the University of South Carolina campus. Extensive collections of gems, minerals, silver pieces, dolls and many art exhibits, some of which are temporary showings.

Time: All year, Mon.-Fri., 9 a.m.-4 p.m.; Sept.-May, Sun. 1-5 p.m.
Place: On corner of Sumter and Pendleton Sts., at the Horse-shoe, on campus.
Contact: (803) 777-7251

Christmas Candlelight Tours

Each year in early December three of Columbia's most attractive, historic homes are decorated as they would have been in the 19th century and lit with thousands of glowing candles. In every room of every home, people dressed in period costumes portray scenes typical of the past, from elegant soirees in formal attire to lively dances and dinners. In four nights the homes use up 5,000 candles—truly a sight worth seeing!

Time: 1st or 2nd week of December, 5:30-8:30 p.m.
Place: Robert Mills, Hampton-Preston, and Woodrow Wilson Boyhood houses.
Contact: (803) 252-7742
Note: Call for directions.

No-Entrance, No-Exit Tunnel

A marvelous *trompe l'oeil* painted by local artist Blue Sky, this tunnel seems real both day and night. It's four stories high and so convincing you may be tempted to drive through it. In fact, it's a solid brick wall.

Place: The north wall of the Farm Credit Bank Bldg., 1401 Hampton St.

Pomp and Pageantry

A thousand soldiers, all spit and polish, are present at the flag lowering ceremony at Fort Jackson each Friday afternoon. Military band music and canon fire add to the aura.

Time: Late Fri. afternoons, weather permitting.
Place: In front of the Headquarters Bldg. at Ft. Jackson.
Contact: (803) 751-6719

Renaissance Art Collection

The Columbia Museum of Art and Science is particularly noted for a superb collection of Renaissance art, 46 works in all, which is on permanent display. The museum also offers rotating exhibits of everything from costumed dolls to mounted African animals.

Time: Tues.-Sat., 10 a.m.-5 p.m.; Sun., 2-6 p.m.
Place: 1112 Bull St.
Contact: (803) 799-2810

Trinity Cathedral

Located across from the State House for which it served as a chapel, the cathedral was built in 1846 as a small-scale replica of Yorkminster Cathedral in Great Britain. The stained-glass windows, including the rose window, were imported from Munich, Germany. In the off-season you can take in special musical events on Wednesday afternoons. Don't miss the historic graveyard as well.

Time: Cathedral: Mon.-Fri., 9 a.m.-5 p.m.; Sat.-Sun., 9 a.m.-noon. Special music events: Wed., 12:30-1 p.m.
Place: 1100 Sumter St. at Senate St.
Contact: (803) 771-7300

Conway

Tobacco Auctions

Close to 12 million pounds of tobacco are sold in the warehouses of Conway each year from July to September. Buyers walk behind the auctioneer, who sells the crop that's stacked on the concrete floors of huge metal buildings. The sight and smell of tobacco and the sound of staccato chants make an auction a memorable experience.

Time: 9 a.m.-2 p.m., on varying weekdays from July to Sept.
Place: In any of 4 warehouses in Conway.

SOUTH CAROLINA

Conway

Contact: Chamber of Commerce, 203 Main St, P.O. Box 831, Conway, SC 29526; (803) 248-2273.
Note: The Chamber keeps auction dates and addresses on hand at all times.

Darlington

Stock Car Hall of Fame

Hot rodders' hearts will throb at the sight of the racing machines of Fireball Roberts, Richard Petty, Buddy Baker, David Pearson and Herb Thomas. There is even a simulated two-lap ride over the hallowed asphalt lanes of Darlington Raceway in "King Richard's Dodge."
Time: 9 a.m.-5 p.m.
Place: W of town on SC 34/151.
Contact: (803) 393-4041

Gowensville

Campbell's Covered Bridge

Built in 1909 over Beaverdam Creek in northern Greenville County, this scenic covered bridge is the only one in the state which still carries traffic.
Place: .25 mi. S of SC 414 and 2.25 mi. E of SC 101. Follow the signs from SC 101.

Greenville

Peaceful Vista

This outdoor chapel, aptly called "Pretty Place," is on a mountainside. It overlooks River Falls Valley, with range after range of Blue Ridge Mountains.
Place: Atop Standing Stone Mountain, off US 276 in the YMCA camp.

Sacred Art Museum

One of the most important art collections in the Southeast. European art from the 13th through 19th centuries is displayed in 30 rooms of the Bob Jones University Museum of Sacred Art. Priceless Rubens, Titians and Tintorettos as well as the Bowen Bible Lands Collection can be seen.
Time: Tues.-Sun., 2-5 p.m. Tours Sept.-May only.
Place: On Wade Hampton Blvd. (US 29).
Contact: (803) 242-5100, ext. 2701.
Note: No children under 6; children 6-12 with adult.

Greenwood

Park Seed Company Gardens

Park is one of the country's largest seed supply houses,

and its test gardens, display plots and greenhouses are open to the public free of charge throughout the year. The annual Flower Day is held in mid-July each year, when the gardens reach their peak in a full palette of color.
Time: Company: 8 a.m.-4:30 p.m.; gardens always visible. Best time in the days before annual Flower Day in mid-July.
Place: 6 mi. N of town on SC 254.
Contact: (803) 374-3341

Hartsville

Nuclear Information Center

Free films and exhibits explain how different fuels are used to generate electricity. There's even a bicycle rigged up to show you how much body energy is required to create a penny's worth of power. The center rests on the site of the first commercial nuclear plant in the Southeast and is by a lake open for recreational use.

Time: Mon.-Fri., 9 a.m.-5 p.m.
Place: 4 mi. NW of town off SC 151.
Contact: (803) 332-2633

Kings Creek

Casting the First Stone

Join others who toss stones on the grave of British Major Patrick Ferguson at Kings Mountain National Military Park. He threatened to lay waste the area, only to be killed by rock-throwing Americans in the Revolution. Also visit the "Living Farm," a homestead typical of the frontier.

Time: 9 a.m.-5 p.m.
Place: Between Charlotte and Spartanburg, four mi. S of exit 2 off I-85, on SC 216.
Contact: (803) 936-7508

Lake City

Truluck Vineyards

Nestled between soybean and tobacco fields, the vineyard is like a touch of France and is the first of its kind in South Carolina. Family-owned and -run, the winery is open for tours and wine tasting for the red, rosé and white table wines.

Time: Tues.-Sat., 10:30 a.m.-5:30 p.m.
Contact: (803) 389-3400

McBee

Wildlife Haven

The Carolina Sandhills National Wildlife Refuge is covered with longleaf pines and scrub oaks, and is the home of white-tailed deer (seen early morning and late evening), 80 colonies of red-cockaded woodpeckers, and the extremely rare pine barrens tree-frog. If you ask where to look, you can also see a variety of pitcher plants. From December to March, 25,000 ducks make the refuge their home. Of interest: a five-mile hiking trail, a paved auto route, two observation towers, picnic areas, and a photography blind in one of the impoundments.

Time: Sunrise to sunset.
Place: 4 mi. N of town on US 1.
Contact: (803) 335-8401

Myrtle Beach

Fifty Miles of Free Beach

All South Carolina beaches are open to the public free of charge. The granddaddy of them all is "The Grand Strand," which runs along the coast for 50 miles, from just south of the North Carolina border. On this stretch lies Myrtle Beach, one of the most popular (and crowded) along the coast. If you prefer isolation, you can find it just by seeking it out.

Orangeburg

Warmwater Fish Hatchery

The Orangeburg National Fish Hatchery works only with warmwater fish, some 25 to 30 species including striped bass, catfish, and sunfish. There are 10 aquariums on display, the largest a 450-gallon monster. Don't miss the alligator—and a dozen of his wild cousins in the pond (they're shy but do appear regularly).

Time: 7:30 a.m.-4:30 p.m.
Place: On US 21, at the bypass south of town.
Contact: (803) 534-4828

SOUTH CAROLINA

Orangeburg

Edisto Memorial Gardens

From a small tract of swamp-land in 1927 these lovely gardens have grown to cover 75 acres with moss-draped trees and blooming shrubs. Azalea, dogwoods, crepe myrtle and wisteria line trails and delight visitors with fragrant scents and colorful blossoms. And over 6,000 roses bloom in season.

Place: On US 301.
Contact: (803) 534-6376
Note: Azaleas peak in Apr.

Parris Island

Marine Corps Recruit Depot

A gardened community with a small-town feeling but with an under-current of rigorous training as men are made into Marines during a grueling 11-week training period. You're allowed to watch much of this by roaming relatively freely (within reason) around the depot. A museum spells out the trials of becoming a Marine and houses a wide collection of military memorabilia.

Time: Museum: 8 a.m.-4:30 p.m.; training best seen in early part of day. Dress parades: 1-3 times a week, 9-9:45 a.m. (call for schedule).
Place: 5 mi. S of Beaufort on SC 281.
Contact: (803) 525-2111 (ask for public affairs officer).

Sassafras Mountain

Highest Point

Sassafras Mountain in Pickens County is the highest point (3,548 feet) in South Carolina. A wonderful view.

Place: Take US 178 near the state line, then right on SC 39/199.

Seneca

Energy Education Center

Everything has been updated in the Keowee Toxaway Visitor Center, which offers a tour of animated displays, some of which invite your participation. Kids enjoy the fission chamber, while older people like to match wits with a computer in an energy quiz.

Time: Mon.-Sat., 9 a.m.-5 p.m.; Sun., noon-5 p.m.
Place: 8 mi. N of town on SC 130.
Contact: (803) 882-5620

Summerville

Old Dorchester State Park

Congregationalists from Massachusetts settled on this bluff overlooking the Ashley River in 1696, but mysteriously abandoned the community in 1778. Today visitors can picnic among the ruins of the parish church tower and the distinctly southern tabby walls of the old fort. Relics are on display.

Place: On SC 642, 6 mi. S of town.
Contact: (803) 873-1740

Sumter

Swan Lake Iris Gardens

Dozens of swans drift lazily by in a setting which is now world-famous for its multiple beds of Japanese iris—hundreds of thousands of them—which burst into bloom from late May to early July.

Time: 8 a.m.-sunset.
Place: W. Liberty St.
Contact: (803) 773-9363

Sunset

Cherokee Indian Artifacts

The Keowee Toxaway State Park lies in a region which was

once the center of the lower Cherokee Indian civilization. Indian artifacts and graphic displays describing Cherokee life are found in the park's interpretive center.

Time: Center: Tues.-Sun., 10 a.m.-5 p.m.
Place: 3 mi. W of town, on Hwy. 11.
Contact: (803) 868-2605

Walhalla

Abandoned Tunnel

The Blue Ridge Railroad began cutting a tunnel through Stumphouse Mountain in the 1850s but went bankrupt in the process, leaving a gaping 1,600-foot long hole. Explore

the tunnel, picnic nearby, and don't miss Issaqueena Falls, a beautiful splashing cascade which drops 200 feet to the valley floor.

Place: Off SC 107. Ask locally for directions.

Walhalla National Fish Hatchery

The hatchery is near a national forest recreation area with picnic grounds. Over a million rainbow, brook and brown trout are raised here for stocking waters in several southern states each year..

Time: 8 a.m.-4 p.m.
Place: N of town on Hwy. 28, then right on SC 107 for approx. 11 mi. Follow signs to hatchery.
Contact: (803) 638-2866

Yemassee

Ruins of Sheldon Church

In this remote setting an Anglican church was built in 1753, only to be burned once in the War of Independence and again in the Civil War. Live oaks, shrouded in Spanish moss, shade ruins of massive

walls and tall columns reminiscent of a Greek temple.

Place: .5 mi. off US 17 on SC 21.
Note: Memorial services held here every year on 2nd Sun. after Easter.

Statewide

Crabbing

All you need is a line, a weight and some chicken backs or necks to go out crabbing. It's one of the most enjoyable pastimes for kids and adults alike—and the catch is delicious. Ask the locals to explain how! Also free are all the oysters, clams, saltwater fish and shrimp you catch.

Time: Crabs and shrimp: all year (shrimping best May-mid-Oct.). Oysters: mid-Sept.-Apr. Clams: Sept.-May.
Place: Crabbing and shrimping along 2,876 miles of tidal shoreline. Gather oysters and clams at State Shellfish Grounds: Alligator Creek, Hamlin Creek, Folly River, Cole Creek, Toogoodoo Creek, Lucy Point Creek, Distant Creek, Old House Creek, Capers Creek, Station Creek, Marsh Island, Habersham Creek, Parris Island, Euhaw Creek.
Contact: Recreational Fisheries, P.O. Box 12559, Charleston, SC 29412; (803) 795-6350 (ask for recreational fisheries).

TENNESSEE

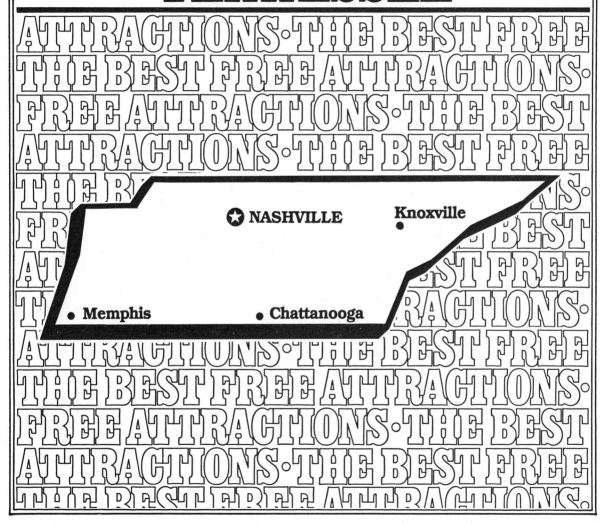

ATTRACTIONS·THE BEST FREE
THE BEST FREE ATTRACTIONS·
FREE ATTRACTIONS·THE BEST
ATTRACTIONS·THE BEST FREE
THE BEST FREE ATTRACTIONS·
FREE ATTRACTIONS·THE BEST
ATTRACTIONS·THE BEST FREE
THE BEST FREE ATTRACTIONS·
FREE ATTRACTIONS·THE BEST
ATTRACTIONS·THE BEST FREE
THE BEST FREE ATTRACTIONS·

★ NASHVILLE

Knoxville

Memphis

Chattanooga

TENNESSEE

Chattanooga

Shoulder Arms Collection

The world's most complete collection of shoulder arms (more than 350) are found at Chickamauga-Chattanooga National Military Park, the nation's oldest, largest and most visited park of its kind. They're in the Fuller Gun Museum, showing the development of weapons from flintlocks to modern models. Tours of the scattered battle sites take you through history and interesting terrain, but are best after a 20-minute program in the visitor center.
Time: June-Sept., 8 a.m.-5 p.m.; rest of year, 8 a.m.-4:45 p.m.
Place: 7 mi. S of town, off US 27.
Contact: (404) 866-9241

Southern Cemetery

The Chattanooga National Cemetery is one of the most beautiful in the South and dates back to 1863. If you're interested in stone rubbings, ask for permission or stop at the smaller, more out-of-the-way cemeteries common in smaller towns.
Time: 8 a.m.-5 p.m.
Place: Off Bailey Ave., E of Central Ave.
Contact: (615) 698-4981

Hunter Museum of Art

In a turn-of-the-century Edwardian mansion surrounded by a hand-sculpted steel fence is a fine collection of American art running through the late 1800s. Works by Alexander Calder, Salvadore Dali and other great artists can also be viewed. In the new building nearby you'll find changing exhibits.
Time: Tues.-Sat., 10 a.m.-4:30 p.m.; Sun., 1-4:30 p.m.
Place: 10 Bluff View.
Contact: (615) 267-0968

Cleveland

Indian Village

The Red Clay State Historic area is being recreated, much as the Cherokee Indians knew it before their infamous removal to Oklahoma. The area includes a reconstructed Indian village and a model Cherokee farm. There's even a replica of a Council House, where political and religious gatherings took place. A ten-minute slide show is included in your visit.
Time: Visitor center: 8 a.m.-4:30 p.m. Park: 8 a.m.-sunset.
Place: 12 mi. S of town, on TN 11 (Blue Springs Rd.). Marked by signs.
Contact: (615) 472-2627

White Water

In the Cherokee National Forest you'll find 500 miles of hiking trails, including 190 miles of the Appalachian Trail—one of the finest trails in the US. If you camp in primitive areas, there's no charge. And the Ocoee River is one of the best white water rafting areas in the South.
Contact: US Forest Service, P.O. Box 400, Cleveland, TN 37311; (615) 476-5528.

Columbia

Mule Day

Thousands of spectators, participants and mules join in for the festivities of "Mule Day," a weekend celebration honoring these beasts of burden. Most of the activities are free, including the liar's contest, the mule sale and the big parade.
Time: 1st weekend in Apr.
Place: Parade on W. Seventh St.
Contact: (615) 388-2155

Dayton

Monkey Trial

The red-brick Rhea County Courthouse in 1925 was the scene of an epic media event, pitting golden-tongued William Jennings Bryan against Clarence Darrow in the Scopes trial. Scopes was accused of teaching Darwinian theory in violation of Tennessee statute. Although the schoolteacher defended by Darrow lost the case, Bryan's arguments defending the fundamentalist view of the creation were demolished and Bryan died in Dayton five days after the trial. Call ahead if you'd like to see a ten-minute film on the trial.

Time: Mon.-Sat., 8:30 a.m.-4 p.m. (closes Wed. and Sat. at noon).
Place: Market St.
Contact: (615) 775-9661

Dover

Rifle and Cannon Firing

It was at Fort Donelson that Ulysses S. Grant demanded an "unconditional and immediate surrender." Although earthworks are all that remain, there is a 15-minute slide program that outlines the Civil War battle. Uniformed interpreters conduct rifle- and cannon-firing throughout the summer and on request.

Time: June-Aug., 8 a.m.-6 p.m.; rest of year, 8 a.m.-4:30 p.m.
Place: 1 mi. W of Dover on US 79.
Contact: (615) 232-5706

Elizabethton

Acres of Rhododendrons

Roan Mountain, with 600 acres of colorful pink and purple rhododendrons, is said to be the largest concentration of these flowering shrubs in the world.

Time: Usually in full bloom from June 20-30.
Place: 20 mi. SE of Elizabethton, off US 19E via TN 137.

Nature Films

Although it's not on its original site, Fort Watauga represents an authentic replica of the original buildings constructed here in the 1800s. Three films, each lasting 35 minutes, may be requested at any time. The museum houses artifacts such as spinning wheels, lumbering tools and looms. A short foot-trail and picnic grounds are also available in this spot, known as Sycamore Shoals.

Time: Sunrise-sunset.
Place: In town on TN 321.
Contact: (615) 543-5808

Gatlinburg

Free Trolley

If you're staying at a hotel or campground in Gatlinburg,

ask for tokens which allow you to take the local trolleys for free. There is no limit on the number of tokens to be used in a day. If you're just passing through, the trolley ride costs a dime.

Appalachian Trail

The Appalachian Trail stretches for 2,015 miles across 12 states, linking Maine with Georgia. The most spectacular portion crosses Great Smoky Mountains National Park along the Tennessee-North Carolina border. A convenient entrance point to the trail is at

TENNESSEE

Gatlinburg

Newfound Gap, near
Gatlinburg.
Contact: Great Smoky Mountains
National Park, Gatlinburg, TN
37738; (615) 436-5615.

800 Miles of Trails

The Appalachian Trail accounts for only 68 miles of the
850 miles of hiking trails in
this national park, a backpacker's dream. Serious hikers
will follow the rugged trail to
the Chimneys, where they'll
have a panoramic view. Contact the park for maps and
suggestions on equally stunning paths.
Contact: Great Smoky Mountains
National Park, Gatlinburg, TN
37738; (615) 436-5615.

Botanists' Paradise

Clouds appear to hang perpetually over the peaks of these
mountains, which the Indians
dubbed the Smokies. In this
moist environment grow more
than 1,300 species of flowering
plants, 350 mosses and liverworts, 230 lichens and thousands of varieties of fungus—
not to mention 100 different
types of trees.
Contact: Great Smoky Mountains
National Park, Gatlinburg, TN
37738; (615) 436-5615.

Blueberry Picking

Wild blueberries are plentiful
throughout this area, and they
can be found at varying elevations which cause them to
ripen at different times
throughout the summer.
You're free to pick and eat as
many as you can find!
Time: July-mid-Aug. (Berries
ripen earliest in low areas.)
Place: Great Smoky Mountains
National Park. Ask locally for
spots approaching their
prime season.
Contact: (615) 436-5615

Great Smoky Mountains

So beautiful are these mountains that a slice 54 miles long
and 19 miles wide has been set
aside as a national park, one of
the most famous and frequently visited of all the parks in the
US. From early June to mid-July the wild azaleas and rhododendrons are ablaze in color,
as are the woods in October
when the leaves turn. Don't
miss the views from Newfound
Gap and Clingmans Dome.
Time: May-Oct., 8 a.m.-9 p.m.;
rest of year, 8 a.m.-4:30 p.m.
Place: Visitor center at Sugarlands, 2.5 mi. SW of town.
Contact: (615) 436-5615

Golden Pond

Living History Farm

The Homeplace is a living-history farm. Scattered
throughout the valley are 16
structures, including log cabins, barns and cribs. Herds of
buffalo graze peacefully in
open fields. Oxen sun themselves in post-and-rail corrals.
And the farms produce crops
of corn—all as they did in the
1850s.
Time: Mar.-Nov., Wed.-Sun., 9
a.m.-5 p.m.
Place: 11 mi. S of town on the
Trace (local hwy.).
Contact: (502) 924-5602

Greeneville

Tailor Shop

Andrew Johnson's tailor shop,
his home on Main Street and
the National Cemetery at the
end of Monument Avenue
make up this national historic
site. Everything is free with the
exception of visits to the house
from June to mid-September,
for which there is a small
charge.
Time: 9 a.m.-5 p.m.
Place: Tailor Shop: Depot and
College Sts.
Contact: (615) 638-3551

TENNESSEE

Jonesboro

Historic Drive
Pick up a free walking and driving tour brochure to get the most from the heart of this town. It represents two centuries of history and architectural styles. The Chester Inn, built in 1797, is the oldest structure and has been in continuous use for 175 years.

Contact: Visitor Bureau, P.O. Box 375, Jonesboro, TN 37659; (615) 753-5961.

Knoxville

Dogwood Arts Festival
Celebrating the whites and pastel pinks of the dogwoods in full bloom, Knoxville sponsors 250 events in one of the South's great festivals. Most of these special events are free, including bus tours along the Dogwood Trails. Band students (12,000 of them!) perform in the largest band competition in the US. Daily live performances, from ballet to bluegrass, occupy the stage of the Market Square Mall.

Time: Late Apr. Mall events: 10 a.m.-3 p.m. Call contact for bus tour information.
Place: Market Sq. Mall.
Contact: Dogwood Arts Festival, P.O. Box 2229, Knoxville, TN 37901; (615) 637-4561.

Art Reproductions
The Frank H. McClung Museum has a collection of fine reproductions, both antiques and paintings. These were commissioned at the turn-of-the-century and contain replicas of works in the Louvre and other major museums. Also featured are natural science exhibits, eastern Tennessee history and changing shows. Don't miss the new gallery across the street with complementary exhibits.

Time: Mon.-Fri., 9 a.m.-5 p.m.
Place: Circle Park, University of Tennessee campus.
Contact: (615) 974-0111

Miniature Rooms
The Dulin Gallery of Art, housed in a mansion, features nine miniature rooms with a one-inch-to-the-foot scale. Rooms reflect diverse cultures and include European and American decor.

Time: Tues.-Fri., noon-4 p.m.; Sat.-Sun., 1-5 p.m.
Place: 3100 Kingston Pike.
Contact: (615) 525-6101

Brown Bag Specials
Bring your lunch to Market Square Mall and enjoy free music throughout the summer! Since schedules and events change yearly, get in touch with the contact for up-to-the-minute information.

Contact: Knox Events Calendar, Area Council for Conventions and Visitors, P.O. Box 15012, Knoxville, TN 37901; (615) 523-7263.

Lebanon

Largest Red Cedar Forest
Said to be the world's largest red cedar forest, this area lies in Cedars of Lebanon State Park (which covers 8,887 acres). Free slide programs are given in different parts of the park throughout the summer, and there are changing exhibits in the visitor center.

Time: Visitor center: 9 a.m.-5 p.m.
Place: 6 mi. S of town on US 231.
Contact: (615) 444-5503

Lynchburg

Jack Daniel Distillery
Although there's no drinking of hard liquor allowed in this county, the one-hour tour of the nation's oldest distillery is

TENNESSEE

Lynchburg

a must. (It was granted Whiskey License No. 1.) After a short film, men like Garland Dusenberry and Yodeler Brannon explain the century-old charcoal process of making Jack Daniel whiskey. At the end of the tour you're offered fresh lemonade at the visitor center. After the late morning tour, some visitors are invited to enjoy a free lunch in a local restaurant.

Time: 8 a.m.-4 p.m.
Place: .25 mi. NE of town on TN 55.
Contact: (615) 759-4221, ext. 312

Manchester

Mystery Park

The Middle Woodland Indians probably built the rock and earthen walls of Old Stone Fort between 30 and 430 A.D. But why they did so is still a mystery. The walls, 4,600 feet in combined length, enclose an area lying between the forks of the Duck and Little Duck Rivers with 60- to 100- foot bluffs on both sides.

Time: 8 a.m.-sunset.
Place: 1.5 mi. N of town off US 41.
Contact: (615) 728-0751

Memphis
Great Getaway

The Memphis Botanic Garden is a great getaway in the cold winter months. Here you'll find a tropical conservatory with everything from rare orchids to banana trees. During the summer the 88 acres of outdoor gardens come into their own with 14 specific divisions, ranging from rose to Japanese gardens.

Time: Mar.-Sept., Mon.-Fri., 9 a.m.-5 p.m.; Sat.-Sun., 1-5 p.m. Rest of year, Mon.-Fri., 9 a.m.-4:30 p.m.; Sat.-Sun., 1-4:30 p.m.
Place: In Audubon Park, at 750 Cherry Rd.
Contact: (901) 685-1566

Brewery Tour

Sample Schlitz beer in a re-created riverboat. It's a fitting close to a 30-minute tour of the brewery.

Time: Mon.-Fri., 10:30 a.m.-3:30 p.m., on the half hour.
Place: 5151 E. Raines Rd.
Contact: (901) 362-5450, ext. 331 or 332

Bluegrass

The Lucy Opry presents bluegrass music in its purest form. People who love to play and love to listen congregate here on Friday nights. In the parking lot, groups tune up and rehearse before their turns onstage. And there's no charge to get inside—just a bucket passed for donations!

Time: Fri., 8 p.m.
Place: Forest Drive Civic Club, 869 Fite Rd.
Contact: (901) 358-3486

May Festivals

May's the big festival month in Memphis, with five free festivals—one for every weekend during the month. Since these vary considerably each year, write or call the contact for an up-to-date schedule of places and times.

Contact: Memphis in May International Festival, Inc., Suite 1224, 12 S. Main St., Memphis, TN 38103; (901) 525-4611.

Shelby Cotton Company

A working exhibit of the processing and selling of cotton, from seed to shirt. The 12-minute tours take you to a grading room with cotton samples in full view. People here are extremely knowledgeable about cotton and enjoy talking about it.
Time: 8:30 a.m.-6 p.m.
Place: 48 S. Front St.
Contact: (901) 526-3157

Zoo and Aquarium

Definitely worth going to are the Memphis Zoo and Aquarium. The latter is the one and only in the mid-South. The zoo is the first in the world to breed gorillas artificially and has the reputation of producing more hippos than any other (47 in 70 years). Don't miss a chat with the myna bird whose extensive vocabulary and wolf whistles will make you smile.
Time: Sat., 9 a.m.-10 a.m. (Open Sun.-Fri., 9 a.m.-5 p.m., but fees charged.)
Place: Overton Park.
Contact: (901) 726-4775

Hands On

The Memphis Museum is a lively place to visit. The museum has an insect zoo of living insects, a tree house for kids to climb, an earthquake exhibit (step on a platform to feel the vibrations as buildings crumble in front of you) and 50 stuffed birds (push buttons to hear them sing).
Time: Sat., 9-10 a.m. (Fees charged at other times.)
Place: 3050 Central Ave.
Contact: (901) 454-5600

Art Gallery

The Brooks Memorial Art Gallery has a portion of the Kress collection of medieval art, Meissen figurines and a schedule of events including free films, concerts and lectures on Sunday. Write for a brochure with a listing of these.
Time: Tues.-Sat., 10 a.m.-5 p.m.; Sun., 1-5 p.m.
Place: Overton Park.
Contact: (901) 726-5266

Magevney House

A simple attraction, this was the home of one of the first schoolteachers in Memphis and dates back to 1837. The one-story house, built partly of logs, is furnished with original possessions of Eugene Magevny. Outside are small gardens.
Time: Tues.-Sat., 10 a.m.-4 p.m.; Sun., 1-4 p.m.
Place: 198 Adams Ave.
Contact: (901) 526-4464

Murfreesboro

Cannon Firing Course

Push a button to start a film which gives you a mini-course in firing a Civil War cannon at Stones River National Battlefield. During the summer, uniformed soldiers fire muskets and cannons regularly. Throughout the year there's an 18-minute film on the battle which resulted in 23,000 casualties. Two tour routes of two to five miles take you past many of the major battle sites and make a fine hike for those interested.
Time: June-Aug., 8 a.m.-8 p.m.; Sept.-May, 8 a.m.-5 p.m.
Place: US 41/70S, NW corner of town.
Contact: (615) 893-9501

Connonsburgh

A village of reconstructed buildings, from a blacksmith shop and grist mill to a town hall and country store.
Time: May-Oct., Tues.-Sat., 10 a.m.-4:30 p.m.; Sun., 1-4:30 p.m.
Place: S. Front St.
Contact: (615) 893-6565

TENNESSEE

Nashville

Parthenon Replica

Nashville, "The Athens of the South," has its own Parthenon, a full-size replica of the original, but in concrete (not hand-carved marble). In the basement is a permanent collection of American painting from 1850 to 1925.

Time: Tues.-Sat., 9 a.m.-4:30 p.m.; Sun., 1-4:30 p.m.
Place: 2 mi. W of town on West End Ave., in Centennial Park.
Contact: (615) 259-6358

Last Supper Woodcarving

Made of limewood and walnut, this 8-foot-high and 17-foot-long woodcarving of *The Last Supper* is the work of Ernest Pellegrini and is displayed in the Upper Room Chapel along with tapestries.

Time: 8 a.m.-4:30 p.m.
Place: 1908 Grand Ave.
Contact: (615) 327-2700, ext. 414

Crown Jewel

Resting on the highest hill in Nashville is the State Capitol, an architectural jewel with a lovely interior. The architect must have sensed that this was a success, for he requested that he be buried in the building after he died.

Time: Tours: 9 a.m.-4 p.m., on the hour.
Place: Charlotte Ave.
Contact: (615) 741-3211

Free Concerts

Up to seven thousand people take advantage of the free concerts at the Band Shell of Centennial Park. Programs range from bluegrass to symphonic, attracting music-lovers of all stripes. Benches are provided, but the atmosphere is so casual that many people bring blankets to lie on.

Time: Mem. Day-Labor Day, Sun., afternoons (call for exact times).
Place: Centennial Park.
Contact: (615) 259-6399
Note: Concert calendars available from Public Information Office, Centennial Park, Nashville, TN 37201.

Oak Ridge

Must Stop

Hundreds of models, gadgets and machines fill eight exhibits that emphasize peacetime use of the atom, in what was once a super secret World War II research center. In the American Museum of Science and Energy you can detect art forgeries using radio-isotopes or track down a radioactive fish in a small aquarium. Then match wits with a computer or view a not-so-peaceful film on the development of atomic weapons.

Time: June-Aug., Mon.-Sat., 9 a.m.-6 p.m.; Sun., 12:30-6 p.m. Rest of year, Mon.-Sat., 9 a.m.-5 p.m.; Sun., 12:30-5 p.m.
Place: .25 mi. W of town via S. Tulane Ave., between TN 62 and TN 95.
Contact: (615) 576-3200

Oneida

Primitive Wilderness

Much of the area is covered with pines and deciduous trees clinging to the slopes along river areas. There's free primitive camping and scenic stretches of river with on-again-off-again white water. For a brochure on the Big South Fork National River and Recreation Area or the Obed Wild and Scenic River, write or call the contact below.

Contact: National Park, P.O. Box 630, Oneida, TN 37841; (615) 569-6389.

Pigeon Forge

Pottery

Not a big place, but popular with pottery people who will be given a tour that's keyed to

110

their particular interest. You can see much of the process, from pots being thrown to glazing.

Time: Apr.-Dec., 8 a.m.-6 p.m.
Place: 1 blk. off US 441, on Middle Creek Rd.
Contact: (615) 453-3883

Pikeville

Fall Creek Falls

The 256-foot drop of Fall Creek Falls makes them the highest east of the Rockies. You'll find them in a park of the same name, which has trails and a nature center as well.

Time: Sunrise-sunset.
Place: NW of town, off TN 30.
Contact: (615) 881-3241

Savannah

National Military Park

A ten-mile tour route takes you to the most significant points of Shiloh National Military Park. The North suffered 13,047 casualties, the South 10,699, in a fierce Civil War confrontation here. A 25-minute film describing the battle gives an excellent overview and makes a tour of the area more meaningful. Note that many visitors miss the

Indian mounds, a secondary attraction.

Time: June-Aug., 8 a.m.-6 p.m.; rest of year, 8 a.m.-5 p.m.
Place: 10 mi. SW of town, on TN 22.
Contact: (901) 689-5275

Shelbyville

Walking Horse Capitol

It's said that you can ride a Tennessee walking horse with a glass of water in your hand and never spill a drop. Shelbyville lays claim to being the "Walking Horse Capitol of the World" and by the number of white-fenced farms in the area, you'll probably agree. To get

past the gates simply call ahead to one of the farms listed as contacts below.

Contact: Bailey-Montgomery: (615) 684-4757. Toby Green: (615) 684-5572. Shadow Valley: (615) 739-2325. Bobo and Sons: (615) 294-5131.

Smithville

Old Time Fiddlers' Jamboree

A musical happening, with music everywhere. Banjos, guitars, spoons—you name it—as well as square dancing and clogging. There's always somebody warming up or performing to appreciative listeners who gather spontaneously. For more polished performances, watch the main competition on a platform set up in front of the local courthouse.

Time: July 4th weekend.
Place: Dekalb County Courthouse.
Contact: (615) 597-5177

Springfield

Tobacco Auctions

Dark-fired tobacco, ten million pounds of it, changes hands in this area each year. Try to show up early at one of the warehouse auctions to see most of the action. Check with

TENNESSEE

Springfield

the contact or in the local paper for times and places of daily sales, which usually occur from late November to mid-March.

Time: Late Nov.-mid-Mar. Arrive no later than 9 a.m.
Place: Warehouses throughout the city.
Contact: Hancock Loose Floor Co., Fifth Ave. E; (615) 384-7444.

Townsend

Living Farm

Two thousand acres are still being farmed at Cades Cove, a living farm that accurately portrays life as it was in a rural area a century ago. The sorghum mill works steadily on weekends from late September through three weekends of October, but during the rest of the year there is always some other activity taking place in many of the buildings scattered over an 11-mile driving tour. (The loop shuts down to car traffic on Saturdays at 6 p.m. It is then open for the evening for bikers only.)

Time: Apr. 15-Oct., sunrise to sunset (closed to cars after 6 p.m. Sat.).
Place: 10 mi. W of town on Laurel Creek Rd.
Contact: (615) 436-5615

Tracy City

Recreation Area

South Cumberland Recreation Area lies in southeastern Tennessee. It offers two separate areas with extensive trail systems. One zone is called the Savage Gulf Natural Area; it takes you into a trail winding through a deep gorge. Don't miss the view from the Stone Door, a 150-foot deep crevice in the crest of the Cumberland Plateau. The second zone, Grundy Forest Natural Area, is worth seeking out for Sycamore Falls. Get full details and a map from the contact below.

Contact: South Cumberland Recreation Area, P.O. Box 1444, Tracy City, TN 37387; (615) 924-2956.

Tullahoma

Whiskey Tour

The Geo. A. Dickel and Co. distillery offers guided tours of its plant, from fermenting vats to wooden barrels and bottling. Tours last about an hour (sorry, no free samples).

Time: Mon.-Fri., 8 a.m.-3 p.m.
Place: 6 mi. N on Cascade Rd.
Contact: (615) 857-3124

Statewide

River Floating

Get a free pamphlet listing 22 rivers suitable for river floating. Tennessee is a state known for its scenic waterways, which often include the thrill of white water.

Contact: Tennessee Department of Tourist Development, 601 Broadway, Nashville, TN 37203; (615) 741-2158.

TEXAS

- Dallas
- ★ AUSTIN
- Houston
- San Antonio

TEXAS

Alamo

Tropical Texas

The 2,000-acre Santa Ana National Wildlife Refuge preserves a remnant of Texas subtropical forest. There are 450 species of plants, two of which are found nowhere else in the state. Of the many varieties of birds, many are of Mexican origin and found nowhere else in the country.

Time: 8 a.m.-6 p.m. Closed when rains wash out roads.
Place: 7.5 mi. S of town on US 281.
Contact: (512) 787-7861

Amarillo

Beef on the Hoof

Every week some 18,000 beef cattle parade through the Amarillo Livestock Auction and are sent to their fate with the bang of the auctioneer's gavel. Outside, the livestock pens cover several acres. Cowboys get from pen to pen by a web of catwalks that stretches above the cattle.

Time: Mon., Tues., 9 a.m.- evening.
Place: 100 S. Manhattan St.
Contact: (806) 373-7464

Austin

Gardens

The Mabel Davis Rose Garden (with 60 varieties of flowers), Taniguchi's Oriental Garden, a Swedish log cabin and a relocated one-room school house—these are all part of the displays at Zilker Garden Center.

Time: Grounds: always open. Visitors' building: Mon.-Fri., 8 a.m.-4:30 p.m.; Sat.-Sun., 2-5 p.m.
Place: 2220 Barton Springs Rd.
Contact: (512) 477-8672

LBJ Library

The Lyndon Baines Johnson Library includes a replica of the Oval Office of the White House as it was in Johnson's day. There is also a film, "The Journey of Lyndon B. Johnson," which tells of the 36th president's political career.

Time: 9 a.m.-5 p.m.
Place: 2313 Red River St.
Contact: (512) 397-5279

State Capitol

Tour the largest state house in the country, an edifice completed in 1888 that is more than 309 feet tall. The capitol is built almost entirely of native materials, from its pink granite exterior walls, to limestone inside walls, to the woodwork in its halls. Many chambers and hallways are furnished with historical paintings.

Time: Tours: 8:30 a.m.-4:30 p.m.
Place: Congress Ave.
Contact: (512) 475-3070

Austwell

Whooping Cranes

From October to early April you stand a good chance of seeing some of the few remaining whooping cranes in the world in Aransas National Wildlife Refuge. The 54,829-acre area is home to more than 70 of the rare birds, which make up one of the last few surviving flocks. There are also white-tailed deer, javelina, armadillos and bobcats. A 40-foot observation tower with spotting scopes makes a great perch for birders.

Time: 8 a.m.-5 p.m.
Place: 7 mi. S of town on FM 2040.
Contact: (512) 286-3559

Bandera

Scenic Drives

Drive several routes through the rolling hills of south-central Texas outside of San Antonio. Small creeks lie in the secluded valleys.

Place: Texas 173 N of town; Texas 173 S of town, Texas 46, and Texas 16 and FM 470.

Beaumont

Babe Zaharias Memorial

The trophies, artifacts, photos and other memorabilia of Mildred "Babe" Didrikson Zaharias, the famous golfer of the 1930s, are on display at this small museum.

Time: 9 a.m.-5 p.m.
Place: Gulf St. and I-10.
Contact: (713) 833-4622

Bonham

Sam Rayburn Library

Sam Rayburn lived in Bonham when he served in Congress as the longest-term Speaker of the House. The library is a collection of his books, papers and historical memorabilia. Rayburn himself contributed the first $10,000 to the construction of the facility.

Time: Mon.-Fri., 10 a.m.-5 p.m.; Sat., 1-5 p.m.; Sun., 2-5 p.m.
Place: W edge of town on US 82.
Contact: (214) 583-2455

Brenham

Making Ice Cream

Watch how ice cream is made and packaged during a tour of the Blue Bell Creameries' ice cream plant. The 25-minute tour takes you through the

supply warehouse, into the processing room where ingredients are mixed and then to the packaging room.

Time: Tues. and Thurs., 10 a.m.
Place: 1000 S. Horton St. (Loop 577).
Contact: (713) 836-7977

Canton

Trade Days

On the weekend that includes the first Monday of every month, fierce trading and bartering takes place across 30 acres of flea markets. Antiques, dogs, poultry and other animals are up for trade during the First Monday Trade Days. A visit here can be as cheap or as expensive as you want to make it.

Time: Fri.-Mon. of 1st weekend in month.
Place: 1 block N of TX 19 on US 64.
Contact: (214) 567-2991

Canyon

Texas History

Indian and prehistoric artifacts, branding irons, paintings and a gun collection at the Panhandle Plains Historical Museum capture the flavor of the settlement of the state. A pioneer village has been re-created on the grounds.

Time: Sept. 1-May 31, Mon.-Sat., 9 a.m.-5 p.m.; Sun., 2-6 p.m. June 1-Aug. 30, Mon.-Sat., 9 a.m.-6 p.m.; Sun., 2-6 p.m.
Place: 2401 Fourth Ave.
Contact: (806) 655-7191

Corpus Christi

Padre Island

Go swimming, sunbathing or beachcombing at the 80-mile long Padre Island National Seashore. Sand dunes shift across the surface of the island. There are hotels, restaurants and other developments on the island, just outside of the designated seashore.

Place: Take John F. Kennedy Causeway onto island, then follow Park Rd. 22.
Contact: (512) 937-2621

Corpus Christi

Port Aransas Ferry

A ferry, which can accommodate your car, departs regularly from Aransas Pass for a 10-minute ride across Gulf waters to Port Aransas and then on a longer cruise to Mustang Island.
Time: Call for schedule.
Place: Aransas Pass waterfront.
Contact: (512) 882-6161

Dallas

Ballet under the Stars

Each autumn, different ballets are presented in several Dallas public parks or plazas—all of them outdoors.
Time: Usually Sept.-Oct.; schedule varies.
Place: Location varies with production.
Contact: (214) 744-4398

CityFest

Concerts—including some by big-name bands—art exhibits, historical exhibits, opera and ballet are just a few of the things you might expect to find throughout downtown Dallas during the annual CityFest.
Time: Oct. Schedule varies year to year.
Contact: (214) 747-8555

Civic Garden Center

Fountains, pools with goldfish and plants of all kinds cover this 7½-acre site. The tropical garden room includes a 20-foot waterfall and tropical trees and plants.
Time: Mon.-Fri., 10 a.m.-5 p.m.; Sat.-Sun., 2-5 p.m.
Place: Forest and First Aves. in Dallas Fair Park.
Contact: (214) 428-7476

Fossils

See the fossilized, mounted bones of a mosasaur, a marine reptile that lived 90 million years ago. Also at the Dallas Museum of Natural History are the bones of a mammoth, displayed now as they would have been found by paleontologists. There are also about 50 dioramas with mounted animals, including a wolf and jaguar.
Time: Mon.-Sat., 9 a.m.-5 p.m.; Sun., noon-5 p.m.
Place: Second and Grand Aves. in Dallas Fair Park.
Contact: (214) 421-2169

Primitive Art

Two collections of the Dallas Museum of Fine Arts bear special attention: a collection of African wooden effigies and painted wood sculpture; and the gold jewlery, goblets and masks that were made in Central and South America before the Spanish conquest. There also are traveling exhibits of sculpture, paintings and photos.
Time: Tues.-Sat., 10 a.m.-5 p.m.; Sun., 1-5 p.m.
Place: Dallas Fair Park.
Contact: (214) 421-4187

Seals and Reptiles

Harbor seals, a 170-pound alligator snapping turtle, small alligators and a variety of salt- and fresh-water fish live at the Dallas Aquarium. Among the fresh-water fish are several game species, including muskies, northern pike, walleye and several varieties of trout.
Time: Mon.-Sat., 9 a.m.-5 p.m.; Sun., 1-5 p.m.

Place: Forest and First Aves. in Dallas Fair Park.
Contact: (214) 428-3587

Shakespeare Festival

Professional actors from New York and Dallas gather at the Fair Park band shell every July to perform Shakespearean plays—and other plays as well.
Time: July evenings; schedule varies.
Place: Second and Forest Aves., Dallas Fair Park.
Contact: (214) 748-6021

Sidewalk Symphony

The Dallas Symphony plays several times every May to a street filled with people. The street is blocked off, tables are set on the pavement, and people bring and eat their lunches while they listen to the music.
Time: May, Wed., noon.
Place: Pacific Ave., from Field St. to Akard St.
Contact: (214) 747-8555

Summertime in the City

The noon concerts in downtown Dallas may be Dixieland jazz, swing dance tunes or Air Force drum and bugle corps marches. But whatever it is, the listening is free during Summertime in the City festivities.
Time: June, Fri., noon.
Place: Plaza of 1 Main Pl.
Contact: (214) 747-8555

Talking Plastic People

Lifesize, talking, transparent people—a man and a woman—explain the intricacies of anatomy to passers-by at the Dallas Health and Science Museum. There also is an energy exhibit that explains, among other things, the story of petroleum. With the completion of another anatomy exhibit in 1982, it will give visitors a "ride through the human body."
Time: Tues.-Sat., 9 a.m.-5 p.m.; Sun., noon-5 p.m.
Place: Forest and First Aves., in Dallas Fair Park.
Contact: (214) 428-8351

Del Rio

Pictographs

If you have a motor boat or canoe with you (and you're willing to paddle your canoe for quite a distance), you can see Indian pictographs in Panther Cave on the Rio Grande. Ask for directions at the headquarters of Amistad National Recreation Area. If you're not ambitious enough to chase after the pictographs, you can boat, swim or fish for bass and catfish. Camping, too, is free.
Place: 3 mi. NW of town on US 90.
Contact: (512) 775-7491

El Paso

Air Defense

The Air Defense Artillery Museum includes exhibits of coastal defense artillery installations that were used in the 19th century through World War II.
Time: Wed.-Sun., 10 a.m.-4:30 p.m.
Place: Pleasanton and Sheridan Rds. in Ft. Bliss.
Contact: (915) 568-4518

Armored Cavalry

The story of the Third Armored Cavalry, the "regiment of mounted rifles," is told in the Third Armored Cavalry Museum. That unit fought in the Mexican War and several Indian campaigns.
Time: Schedule varies.
Place: Bldg. 1014 in Ft. Bliss.
Contact: (915) 568-4518

Chamizal National Memorial

The Chamizal National Memorial, a monument to the century of border clashes between two nations, now stands witness to the cooperation of the United States and Mexico. At this 55-acre site, there is a ring where Mexican rodeos are held, a theater where bi-cultural performances are pre-

TEXAS

El Paso

sented, and a museum where the settlement of the area is depicted.
Time: 8 a.m.-5 p.m.
Place: 800 S. San Marcial St.
Contact: (915) 543-7880

Old Fort Bliss

The century-long history of Fort Bliss is recreated in its Replica Museum, whose exhibits are housed in a recreation of the stronghold as it appeared in 1854.
Time: 9 a.m.-4:30 p.m.
Place: Pleasanton Rd. and Pershing Dr., in Ft. Bliss.
Contact: (915) 568-4518

Fort Davis

Trail through the Hills

A 74-mile loop of roads winds through the rugged outcrops and cliff faces in the Davis Mountains. Many of the big hills, including 8,382-foot Mt. Livermore, are on private land and can be viewed only from the road. The countryside is covered with juniper, pines, oak, mesquite and other brush. The circuit takes you past eight roadside parks.
Place: Start 2 mi. S of town on TX 17, then take TX 166 W and

N to TX 118, then SE to TX 17 and back to Ft. Davis.
Contact: (915) 426-3337

Use a Telescope

With a little forethought, you can tour the W. J. McDonald Observatory and peer through an 82-inch reflecting telescope trained on planets, double stars and nebulae. The telescope is available for public use during the last Wednesday evening of each month, though to use it requires a six-month reservation during the summer and about a three-month notice during the winter. However, connected with the observatory is a small museum of astronomy. It is open more frequently and has slide shows and hourly lectures (and requires no reservations).
Time: Museum: Sept.1-May 31, Mon.-Sat., 9 a.m.-5 p.m.; Sun., 1-5 p.m. June 1-Aug. 31, Mon.-Sat., 9 a.m.-7 p.m.; Sun., 1-7 p.m. Telescope: last Wed. night each month. Reservations required.
Place: 17 mi. NW of Ft. Davis on TX 118.
Contact: (915) 426-3423

Fort Stockton

Stagecoaches

Follow the blue lines on the streets of Fort Stockton to the town's historical district and

then seek out the Annie Riggs Memorial Museum. The building once served as a stop for Overland-Butterfield Stage passengers and now contains its original furnishings, guns, saddles, documents and other items from the past.
Time: Mon.-Tues., Thurs.-Sat., 10 a.m.-noon and 2-5 p.m.
Place: S. Main and Callaghan Sts.
Contact: (915) 336-7106

Fort Worth

Botanic Gardens

More than 3,500 rose bushes and 2,000 other plants (including 150 different kinds of trees) cover the 115-acre Fort Worth Botanic Gardens. Although some of the trees are fruit trees, they are raised for their blossoms, not their fruit. There is also a 7½-acre Japanese garden.
Time: Rose garden: 8 a.m.-dark. Japanese garden: May 1-Labor Day, Tues.-Sat., 9 a.m.-7 p.m.; Sun., 1-6 p.m. Rest of year, Tues.-Fri., 10 a.m.-4 p.m.; Sat., 10 a.m.-5 p.m.; Sun., 1-5 p.m.
Place: NW corner of jct. of I-30 and University Dr.
Contact: (817) 870-7686

Kimbell Art Museum

Art works ranging from those of Stone Age men to those of Picasso are displayed in the

Kimbell Art Museum. The art collection is based on the private collection of Kay Kimbell.
Time: Tues.-Sat., 10 a.m.-5 p.m.; Sun., 1-5 p.m.
Place: W on Will Rogers Rd. to Amon Carter Sq.
Contact: (817) 332-8451

Western Art

Western artists such as Russell and Remington are featured in the Amon Carter Museum of Western Art, which was named for a benefactor to the city. You'll see both traveling and permanent exhibits.
Time: Tues.-Sat., 10 a.m.-5 p.m.; Sun., 1-5:30 p.m.
Place: 3501 Camp Bowie Blvd.
Contact: (817) 738-1933

Fritch

Flint Quarries

The Alibates Flint Quarries National Monument preserves the area where many generations of prehistoric people collected the stone from which they fashioned their spear points. The area is also the site of ancient villages and prehistoric petroglyphs. Visitors are admitted only through guided tours, so be sure to make an appointment.
Time: Mem. Day-Sept. 30, 10 a.m. and 2 a.m.; tours by appt. during rest of year.

Place: E edge of Fritch on TX 136.
Contact: (806) 857-3151

Galveston

Ferry

Treat yourself and your car to a two-mile ride over the Gulf waters between Galveston and Bolivar Peninsula.
Time: Departures range from hourly to every 20 minutes, depending on the time of day.
Place: NE end of Galveston Is.
Contact: (713) 763-2386

Hitting the Wall

Perhaps one of the nation's greatest jogs is on the ten-mile Galveston seawall along the Gulf of Mexico. Every mile of the route is marked, and no traffic interferes with the running. You may pant, but you can at least take big lungfuls of the salty sea air.

Harlingen

Ducks, Deer and More

Ducks, shore birds, deer, yucca, cacti and a multitude of other living things can be seen at the Laguna Atascosa National Wildlife Refuge. Boaters can explore the Harlingen Ship

Channel too. What you will see will vary with the season.
Time: Anytime, though bad weather may wash out or flood access roads.
Place: 25 mi. E of town on FM 106.
Contact: (512) 748-3607

Houston

Battle for Independence

The 570-foot tall San Jacinto Monument stands at the site where Texan forces defeated Mexican General Santa Anna's forces and won independence for Texas. Exhibits at the Museum of Texas History trace the area's history from the Spanish conquest of the Indians to Texas's entrance to the Union.
Time: Museum: Tues.-Sun., 9:30 a.m.-5:30 p.m.
Place: From downtown, go 8 mi. S on I-45, 1 mi. N on Loop 610, 11 mi. E on TX 225, 4 mi. N on TX 134.
Contact: (713) 479-2431

Blaffer Gallery

This University of Houston gallery presents classical and modern works—paintings, sculptures and craft shows. Most of the displays are traveling exhibits.
Time: Tues.-Sat., 10 a.m.-6 p.m.; Sun., 1-6 p.m. Gallery closes

TEXAS

Houston

between exhibits, so call ahead.
Place: Fine Arts Bldg. Take Entrance 5 from Cullin Blvd.
Contact: (713) 749-1320

Environmental Zoo

A variety of habitats have been designed to suit their occupants at the Houston Zoo. Tropical birds live in a rain forest and gorillas while away their time in their special gorilla habitat. Watch the feeding of the vampire bats. There also are a reptile house and children's zoo.
Time: 9:30 a.m.-6 p.m.
Place: Fannin St. and Outer Belt Dr. in Hermann Park.
Contact: (713) 523-3211

Houston Festival

Watch more than 3,000 performers present symphony, jazz, ballet, chamber and other varieties of music and dance performances on many different stages and in several parks scattered throughout Houston.
Time: Last 2 weeks in Mar.; schedule varies year to year.
Place: Varies with performances.
Contact: (713) 521-9239

Gulf Port Cruise

Got a dream of being a tugboat captain? Board the *Sam Hous-*

ton and cruise the port of Houston to learn about the bustle of a major harbor.
Time: Tues., Wed., Fri. and Sat., 10 a.m. and 2:30 p.m.; Sun., 2:30 p.m.
Place: 7300 Clinton Dr., gate 8.
Contact: (713) 225-0671
Note: Two-week notice is required for individuals and arrangements for groups must be made two months in advance.

Ima Hogg

A big collection of 17th-, 18th- and early 19th-century furniture, dinnerware, paintings and other appointments are housed in the Bayou Bend Museum, which once was the mansion of Ima Hogg, the daughter of the first native-born Texas governor. Tours last two hours; make a reservation.
Time: Tours: Tues.-Fri., 10 a.m.-2:30 p.m.; Sat., 10-12:45 a.m.
Place: 1 Wescott St.
Contact: (713) 529-8773

Museum of Fine Arts

Paintings by Frederic Remington are among the popular traveling exhibits of the Houston Museum of Fine Arts. The displays are complemented by a garden-level lunchroom, gift shop and public library.
Time: Tues.-Sat., 10 a.m.-5 p.m.; Sun., noon-6 p.m.
Place: 1001 Bissonnet St.
Contact: (713) 526-1361

Museum of Medicine

A see-through mannequin in the Houston Museum of Medical Science lights up every half-hour to show the various functions of the body. The many recordings accompanying the different models and dioramas throughout the museum are read in both English and Spanish.
Time: Sun.-Mon., 4:45 p.m.; Tues.-Sat., 9 a.m.-4:45 p.m.
Place: 5800 Caroline Ave. in Hermann Park.
Contact: (713) 529-3766

Museum of Natural Science

The Houston Museum of Natural Science doesn't specialize; it covers a whole range of times and topics. At one end of the spectrum is a display with moon rocks and other items from space. Another of its 13 large halls features the Age of Dinosaurs. You can also follow the story of oil and the history of Texas.
Time: Tues.-Sat., 9 a.m.-5 p.m.; Sun., Mon., noon-5 p.m.
Place: 1 Hermann Cir. in Hermann Park.
Contact: (713) 526-4273

Outdoor Theater

Opera, symphony, ballet, Broadway musicals, jazz and other kinds of entertainment are performed—free—outdoors while the audience is protected against any bad weather by a big steel canopy. The Miller Outdoor Theater seats 1,350.
Time: Easter-Oct. 31; schedule of individual shows varies.
Place: 100 Concert Dr. in Hermann Park.
Contact: (713) 222-3577

Sam Houston Park

Sam Houston Park, a downtown public park, shows how Houston residents lived during the late 19th century. Though there is a charge to tour some of the old mansions and watch a slide presentation, it costs nothing to stroll by the old homes and other buildings and soak up some Texas history.
Place: Allen Pkwy. and Bagby St.
Contact: (713) 223-8367

Scenic Drive

Take a drive through River Oaks, one of Houston's richest residential neighborhoods, and view antebellum mansions of diverse styles. The area, which is heavily wooded, is most spectacular in March and April when azaleas bloom.
Time: Anytime.
Place: Take Allen Pkwy. along Buffalo Bayou Park.

Space Center

Tour Mission Control of the LBJ Space Center, learn how astronauts are trained and see how space gear is tested for future flights. A big Saturn V plus other rockets and related equipment are on display.
Time: 9 a.m.-4 p.m.
Place: 3 mi. E of I-45 on NASA Rd. 1.
Contact: (713) 483-0123

Huntsville

Sam Houston Park

Several of the homes of Sam Houston, the first president of the Republic of Texas, are in the Huntsville park bearing his name. The homes were relocated and are furnished as they would have been in his time. There also is a museum of early Texas life with exhibits of clothing, weapons, ammunition, carriages and other artifacts of the times.
Time: Mon.-Fri., 8:30 a.m.-5 p.m. Closed noon-1 p.m.
Place: 1327 11th St.
Contact: (713) 295-8113

Johnson City

LBJ's Home

The home and ranch of a former president are preserved in Lyndon B. Johnson National Historical Park. You can see Johnson's boyhood home and the site of his grandfather's cattle-drive operation. Fourteen miles west on U.S. 290, in Stonewall, is the "Texas White House"—Johnson's ranch.
Time: 9 a.m.-5 p.m.; summer hours may be later.
Place: Downtown.
Contact: (512) 868-7128

Kountze

Big Thicket

Twelve units of Big Thicket National Preserve—each an environmental pocket with its own kind of habitat and

TEXAS

Kountze

wildlife—are scattered about eastern Texas. The land is open to visitors at any time, but to find them all—and to keep from getting lost—you need a map from the visitor center.
Time: Visitor center: summer, 9:30 a.m.-5:30 p.m.; winter, Thurs.-Mon., 10 a.m.-4:30 p.m. Definitions of seasons vary yearly, so call ahead.
Place: Visitor center: 7.5 mi. N of town on US 287, then E on FM 420 for 2 mi. Units are scattered in the area.
Contact: Big Thicket National Preserve, P.O. Box 7408, Beaumont, TX 77706; (713) 838-0271.

Lajitas

Canyon Drive

El Camino del Rio—the "River Road"—runs north from Lajitas through the hills and canyons of the region near the Rio Grande.
Time: Anytime.
Place: FM 170 from town.

Langtry

Judge Roy Bean Center

It is said that Judge Roy Bean told actress Lily Langtry that he had named this town after her and thereby expected to win her favor. It was a lie, of course—it was already named Langtry after a civil engineer—but it gives you some idea of the judge's integrity. Among the two most telling exhibits in this museum are Judge Bean's law book and his revolver—the two most important tools of his brand of justice. The exhibits are housed in a visitor center with a replica of the Jersey Lily saloon.
Time: 8 a.m.-5 p.m.
Place: Loop 25 in Langtry.
Contact: (512) 291-3340

Lubbock

Prairie Dogs

At any one time you can see a hundred or more prairie dogs as they whistle warnings and scamper for their burrows. Their 7½-acre town is in Mackenzie State Park.
Time: Daylight hours.
Place: NE of town at I-27 and First St.
Contact: (806) 762-6411

Luckenbach

Something out of Nothing

The four permanent residents of Luckenbach have been overwhelmed by thousands of sightseers ever since Waylon Jennings and Willie Nelson crooned, "Let's go to Luckenbach, Texas" a few years ago. There are a couple of stone buildings, a dance hall and an old general store in town. That's all, most of the year. But thousands of people flow into town during the Luckenbach Chili Cook-off. During the cook-off, you can hear some good music for free, and you might wrangle a spoonful of award-winning chili.
Time: 1st weekend in Oct.
Place: 5 mi. W of Fredericksburg on US 290, then N on RM 1376 for 6 mi., then E on Luckenbach Rd.
Contact: (512) 997-3224

Lufkin

Texas Logging

You can climb a 100-foot fire tower outside of the Texas Forestry Museum. There is also an old logging train with steam locomotive, tender, logging car and caboose. Inside the museum are logging carts and wagons and a scale model of a newsprint mill. Lufkin was

the home of the South's first paper mill.
Time: 1-4:30 p.m.
Place: 1903 Atkinson Dr.
Contact: (713) 634-5523

Luling

Watermelon Thump

The "Thump" is an annual four-day festival in this small Texas town. There is a watermelon-eating contest, a watermelon auction, a fiddle contest, a street dance and the crowning of the Watermelon Thump Queen.
Time: Last weekend in June; schedule varies year to year.
Place: Davis St.
Contact: (512) 875-3214

Marathon

Big Bend National Park

Canyons with sheer cliffs 1,500 feet high and the Rio Grande River are the dominating features in Big Bend National Park. But there is more to this 708,000-acre park than its lands and waters: at some times of the year, there are more than 350 species of birds in the area. There are also more than 100 miles of paved roads and an even greater length of dirt roads in the park.
Time: Visitor center: Labor Day-Mem. Day, 8 a.m.-5 p.m.; rest of year, 8 a.m.-7 p.m.
Place: 80 mi. S of town.
Contact: (915) 477-2251

Nickel Creek

Highest Peak

The highest spot in Texas—8,751-foot Guadalupe Peak—is found in Guadalupe Mountains National Park near the New Mexico border. The real geologic importance of the area, however, is the extent of fossilized rock that was left when the area, now desert, was covered by the sea. Moreover, there are four different climatic zones in the area—from

cacti in the desert region to pines in the highlands and spruce and fir in the higher regions.
Time: Labor Day-May 31, 8 a.m.-4:30 p.m.; rest of year, 8 a.m.-6 p.m.
Place: Visitor center: NW of town, off US 62/180.
Contact: (915) 828-3385

Odessa

Presidential Museum

Constructed after the asassination of President John F. Kennedy, the Presidential Museum is dedicated to the office of the president. It includes displays of 1,000 political cartoons, campaign memorabilia, first-lady dolls with replicas of inaugural gowns and other permanent and changing displays.
Time: Mon.-Thurs. and Sat., 9 a.m.-noon, 1-5 p.m.; Fri., 10 a.m.-noon and 1-5 p.m.
Place: 622 N. Lee St.
Contact: (915) 332-7123

Rockport

Aquarium

Specimens of the fish and other creatures that haunt the Gulf also live in the Marine Laboratories and Aquarium of Texas Parks and Wildlife Department. Species commonly

TEXAS

Rockport

on display are red and black drum, spotted sea trout, southern flounder, sheepshead and octupi. Occasionally sharks and seahorses are added.
Time: Mon.-Fri., 8 a.m.-5 p.m.
Place: Downtown, end of the turning basin.
Contact: (512) 729-2328

San Antonio

Alamo

The Alamo, of course, is the old mission, converted to a fort, where Davy Crockett and James Bowie died and Texas was born. In 1836, the 187 defenders died in their two-week battle against the army of Santa Anna. The Alamo, built by Franciscans in 1744, now houses displays on Texas history.
Time: Mon.-Sat., 9 a.m.-5:30 p.m.; Sun., 10 a.m.-5:30 p.m.
Place: Alamo Plaza and Houston St.
Contact: (512) 225-1391

Circus Displays

The history of the circus is recounted through the Hertzberg Circus Collection. There are photos of circus stars,

memorabilia about Tom Thumb, statues and paintings.
Time: 1st Sun. in May through last Sun. in Oct., Mon.-Sat., 9 a.m.-5:30 p.m.; Sun., 1-5 p.m. Rest of year, Mon.-Sat., 9 a.m.-5:30 p.m.
Place: 210 W. Market St. in Main Library Annex.
Contact: (512) 299-7810

Famous Art

Valuable Picassos and other master works of Mexican, American and European artists are on display at the Marion Koogler McNay Art Institute. Films, lectures and chamber music are frequently scheduled.
Time: Tues.-Sat., 9 a.m.-5 p.m.; Sun., 2-5 p.m.
Place: 6000 N. New Braunfels Ave.
Contact: (512) 824-5368

Free Beer

Stop in at the Jersey Lily Hospitality Center and sip free Pearl beer or soda water. The center, run by Pearl Brewing Co., is housed in a redecorated stable and is named for Lily Langtry, the actress with whom Judge Roy Bean fell in love. There is also a museum with displays of Indian artifacts, Winchester rifles, Colt handguns, a collection of

Bowie knives and a tape about the life of Judge Bean.
Time: Mon.-Fri., 10 a.m.-4 p.m.
Place: 312 Pearl Pkwy.
Contact: (512) 226-0231

Historic District

Drive through the King William Historic District, a neighborhood begun by German immigrants who built mansions and large houses here in the mid-1800s. The architecture is eclectic—Victorian with a lot of other styles thrown in.
Place: 6 blocks off King William's St. from South St. Mary's St. to Guenther St.
Contact: (512) 227-8786

Lackland Air Force Base

See displays of airplane engines that date from the beginning of aviation to the present. There also are wind-tunnel models of various airplanes and dioramas depicting some of the major achievements in aviation.
Time: Mon.-Fri., 8:30 a.m.-4 p.m.; Sat., Sun., 9 a.m.-6 p.m.
Place: SW of airport to US 90 E, exit on Military Dr.
Contact: (512) 671-3444

Mexican Market

Window-shoppers and photographers take note: colorful shops selling imported items

from Mexico—leather goods, glass, pottery and other handicrafts—are located next to a San Antonio farmers market that sells fresh produce. The farmers market is open all the time; the hours of the shops are more restricted.
Time: Shops: 10 a.m.-6 p.m.
Place: Commerce St. and I-35.
Contact: (512) 299-8596

Mexican Village

La Villita is a recreated Mexican Village with narrow streets flanked by patios and authentic adobe houses. This section of town shows a portion of San Antonio as it existed during Texas's fight for independence.
Place: Villita and S. Alamo Sts.

River Music Festival

Every year the residents of San Antonio load a bunch of bands—including some well-known groups—onto barges and let them play for three days on a canal that winds through the downtown. It's called Great Country River Festival and it gives people all the country music they could want. The riverfront is a quaint, enjoyable place even when there is no music.
Time: 1st full weekend in Feb. Schedule varies year to year.
Place: Paseo del Rio, along the San Antonio River.
Contact: San Antonio River

Assn., 306 N. Presa St., San Antonio, TX 78205; (512) 226-2345.

Sunken Gardens

Ponds, waterfalls, footbridges, plus exotic and native ornamental plants surround a Japanese pagoda at the Sunken Gardens in Brackenridge Park. The garden is so named because it seems sunken, surrounded by hills in its San Antonio neighborhood.
Place: N. St. Mary's St. and Mulberry St.
Contact: (512) 299-3215

Texan Cultures

Twenty-seven of the ethnic groups and cultures that helped create Texas are represented in exhibits at the Institute of Texan Cultures. The displays describe the settlers' food, clothing, music, festivals and other aspects of their ways of life.
Time: Tues.-Sun., 9 a.m.-5 p.m.
Place: 801 S. Bowie St. (corner of Durango and I-37).
Contact: (512) 226-7651

Sandia

Thousands of Cows

If you've always wanted to see how to milk 5,000 Jersey cows, stop by the Knolle Jersey Farms, two adjacent farms owned by two brothers. There

are no formal tours, though the owners or workers will show you the barns, the cows and the milking procedure.
Place: 5 mi. E of town on FM 70.
Contact: ((512) 547-2808

Sinton

Wildlife Preserve

The Welder Wildlife Foundation, which owns this huge private preserve, is dedicated to the study and protection of wildlife. On the 7,800-acre site you may see white-tailed deer, wild turkey, javelina, feral hogs and armadillos during a tour of the preserve in a big van. There is also a small museum which explains the purpose and development of the foundation and has displays of mounted animals.
Time: Tour: Thurs., 3 p.m.
Place: 7.3 mi. NE of town on US 77.
Contact: (512) 364-2643

Tyler

Antebellum Museum

Papers, silver and china from the period before and during the Civil War are on display in an antebellum home that forms the Goodman Museum.
Time: 1-4:45 p.m.
Place: 624 N. Broadway.
Contact: (214) 597-5304

TEXAS

Tyler

Biggest Municipal Rose Garden

The 38,000 rose bushes (500 varieties) that cover the 22-acre Tyler Municipal Rose Garden make it the largest city-owned garden of its kind in the country. There also are tall trees, fountains, gazebos, archways and ponds on the grounds.

Time: 8 a.m.-5 p.m.
Place: W. Front St. on East Texas
     Fairgrounds.
Contact: (214) 593-2131

Waco

Robert Browning

The Armstrong Browning Library of Baylor University claims two distinctions: it has the biggest collection of memorabilia of poet Robert Browning, and it has the largest secular collection of stained glass windows. The windows—52 of them, illuminating 6 rooms—depict scenes from Browning's poems.

Time: Mon.-Fri., 9 a.m.-noon, 2-4
     p.m.; Sat., 9 a.m.-noon.
Place: Eighth and Speight Sts.
Contact: (817) 755-3566

VIRGINIA

ATTRACTIONS·THE BEST FREE
THE BEST FREE ATTRACTIONS·
FREE ATTRACTIONS·THE BEST
ATTRACTIONS·THE BEST FREE
THE BEST FREE ATTRACTIONS·
FREE ATTRACTIONS·THE BEST
ATTRACTIONS·THE BEST FREE
THE BEST FREE ATTRACTIONS·
FREE ATTRACTIONS·THE BEST
ATTRACTIONS·THE BEST FREE
THE BEST FREE ATTRACTIONS·

Arlington •

RICHMOND
★

Norfolk •

VIRGINIA

Accotnik

Pohick Church

Founded in 1773, this historic structure was once the parish church of Mount Vernon. George Washington selected the site for the church in 1767 and served as its vestryman for 27 years.
Time: 8 a.m.-4 p.m.
Place: 2 mi. SW of town on US 1.

Alexandria

Stabler-Leadbeater Apothecary Museum

This late 18th-century drug-store was frequented by the likes of George and Martha Washington and Robert E. Lee, and remains in its original condition. The old wooden shelves are stocked with hand-blown glass nursing bottles, "perfection" eyeglasses and many varieties of antique surgical instruments.
Time: Mon.-Sat., 10 a.m.-4:30 p.m.; closed holidays.
Place: 105-107 S. Fairfax St.
Contact: (703) 836-3713

George Washington Bicentennial Center

Two permanent exhibits and several rotating displays present the American Revolution and the history of early plantation life in northern Virginia, through vivid audio-visual commentary. Travel information and a museum gift shop are also at the center.
Time: 9 a.m.-5 p.m.
Place: 201 S. Washington St.
Contact: (703) 750-6677

Washington's Birthday Celebration

Alexandria, the hometown of George Washington, honors his birthday each February with a month-long celebration. The highlight of this event is a gala parade in the city's Old Town district, featuring several fife-and-drum corps, citizens costumed as colonial soldiers and more. Other events can be found all over the city throughout the month.
Contact: (703) 549-0205

Re-fighting the Revolution

One of the most exciting highlights of the month-long Washington's Birthday celebration in Alexandria is the revolutionary war reenactment at Fort Ward Park. Don't miss the mock battle between British and Colonial troops. There's also a fine interpretive program on the life of a typical revolutionary war soldier.
Place: 4301 W. Braddock Rd., about 6 mi. from Washington D.C. via I-395.
Contact: (703) 750-6425
Note: Parking is available on West Braddock Rd.

Fort Stevens Battle Reenacted

Union and Confederate troops clash again during a reenactment of the Battle of Fort Stevens held every August 10 at Fort Ward Park, a 40-acre historic landmark built to protect Washington, D.C. from invasion during the Civil War. The mock battle is part of a two-day Civil War program that includes military unit competition and an authentic war encampment. While here, stop for a picnic on the grounds or walk along the scenic nature trails.
Time: Park: 9 a.m.-sunset. Museum: Tues.-Sat., 9 a.m.-5 p.m.; Sun., noon-5 p.m.

Fort Ward Museum and Park

Located in this 40-acre woodland park is a partial restoration of one of the stone forts built to defend Washington during the Civil War. Those interested in Civil War artifacts should view the cannons, guns and costumes in the Civil War Museum. Interpretive programs are offered in the summer—ask about free concerts.

Time: Park: 9 a.m.-sunset. Museum: Tues.-Sat., 9 a.m.-5 p.m.; Sun., noon-5 p.m. Concerts: mid-May-mid-Sept., Thurs., 7:45 p.m.
Place: 4301 W. Braddock Rd., between King St. and Seminary Rd., just E of I-395.
Contact: (703) 750-6425

Mount Vernon Trail

The 17-mile Mount Vernon Trail runs alongside the Potomac River and George Washington Memorial Parkway from Mount Vernon to the Lincoln Memorial in Washington D.C. Walk, jog or ride your bike past such sites as Fort Hunt Park, Dyke Marsh Wildlife Habitat, a 19th-century lighthouse at Jones Point Park, Lady Bird Johnson Park and the Arlington Memorial Bridge. You might also want to have a picnic on the grass along the way.

Contact: Superintendent, George Washington Memorial Parkway, Turkey Run Park, McLean VA 22101; (703) 426-6600

Christ Church

George Washington and Robert E. Lee both worshiped in this historic church, which has remained virtually unchanged since its construction in the 1770s. Some of the unusual features of the church include the "wine glass" pulpit (shaped like a delicate glass) and the beautiful chandeliers.

Time: Mon.-Fri., 9:30 a.m.-5 p.m.; Sat., 9 a.m.-noon; Sun., 2-4:30 p.m.
Place: 118 N. Washington St., at the corner of Washington and Columbus.
Contact: (703) 549-1450

George Washington Masonic National Memorial

From its site high above the Potomac River, this 333-foot high shrine commands a view of Alexandria at its feet and Washington six miles distant. Inside are numerous "secret" meeting rooms and a chair from which George Washington presided. Children will appreciate the 28-foot long musical toy parade with platoons of nobles marching to recorded band music.

Time: 9:15 a.m.-4 p.m.
Place: King St. and Callahan Dr.
Contact: (703) 683-2007

Arlington

The Pentagon

The Pentagon is the world's biggest office building. Some

27,000 people work here in rooms flanking mile-long corridors often filled with bike-riding messengers. Contained in this famous building are the offices of the armed forces chief, the secretary of defense and colorful displays of trophies, medals, uniforms and battle-action photos.

Time: Mon.-Fri., 7 a.m.-6 p.m.
Place: Across 14th St. Bridge.
Contact: (202) 695-1776

Tomb of the Unknown Soldier

Buried under this famous tomb is the body of an unknown soldier brought back from France after World War I.

VIRGINIA

Arlington

The striking sculpture is carved from a piece of Colorado-Yule marble, one of the largest blocks ever quarried. Also buried here are the remains of unknown American soldiers who died in World War II and the Korean War. Selected members of the military guard the tomb 24 hours a day. The changing of the guard is a ritual worth seeing.

Time: Cemetery: Oct.-Mar. 8 a.m.-5 p.m.; Apr.-Sept., 8 a.m.-7 p.m. Changing of the guard: every half hour during summer; every hour during winter.
Place: Arlington National Cemetery.
Contact: (202) 692-0931

Kennedy Graves

Each year thousands visit the grave of John F. Kennedy, marked by an eternal flame. Adjacent is the gravesite of Robert F. Kennedy.

Time: Oct.-Mar., 8 a.m.-5 p.m.; Apr.-Sept., 8 a.m.-7 p.m.
Place: Arlington National Cemetery.
Contact: (202) 692-0931

Marine Corps War Memorial

At the north end of the cemetery, overlooking the Capital stands this famous memorial depicting the flag-raising at Iwo Jima. Modeled after Joseph Rosenthal's photo, this statue stands 78 feet high and weighs 100 tons. Don't miss the color ceremony and drill by a platoon of marines—and hear a half-hour taped concert of the 49 Netherland bells.

Time: Color ceremony: June 1-Aug. 31, Tues., 7:30 p.m.
Place: Arlington National Cemetery.
Contact: (202) 692-0931

Arlington House

Visit this beautifully restored mansion overlooking the Potomac and the Capital, where Robert E. Lee courted and married Mary Ann Randolph Curtis. They lived here from 1831 to 1861. Because of its location, Union troops occupied the house during the Civil War. It is a 12-minute walk from Arlington Cemetery Visitor Center.

Time: Apr.-Sept., 9:30 a.m.-6 p.m.; rest of year, 9:30 a.m.-4:30 p.m.
Place: Arlington National Cemetery.
Contact: (202) 692-0931

Netherlands Carillon Tower

This striking tower and its 49 bells were a gift from the Netherlands in gratitude for the aid given by the US during and after World War II. Live concerts are performed throughout the year.

Time: Concerts: Sat. and holidays, 2 p.m.
Place: Outside Arlington National Cemetery, on Ridge Rd. off US 50.
Contact: (703) 827-0741

Big Stone Gap

Early Virginia Life

The Southwest Virginia Museum and Historical State Park contain various items and dioramas depicting the history and activities of southwestern Virginia, including pioneer furnishings, folk art and culture and miniature log houses.

Time: Tues.-Sat., 9:30 a.m.-5 p.m.; Sun., 2-5 p.m.
Place: W. First St. and Wood Ave.
Contact: (703) 523-1322

Charlottesville

University of Virginia

Founded by Thomas Jefferson in 1817, this impressive university also bears the stamp of his architectural genius. Many of the old buildings were modeled after classical models, in particular the Rotunda after the Pantheon in Rome. Even more noteworthy is the plan of the quadrangle, which originally housed both students and faculty, and the connecting arcade which wraps the space. The rooms of such famed former students as Edgar Allan Poe and Woodrow Wilson are preserved for public viewing. A Museum of Fine Arts is another attraction on campus.

Time: Mon.-Fri., 11 a.m.-3 p.m.; Sat., 11 a.m., 2 and 4 p.m.; no tours mid-May-mid-Sept., mid-Dec.-mid-Jan. or during exams.

Place: On US 29 and 250 business routes.

Chincoteague

Wallops Flight Center

NASA's Wallops Island facility is a launch site for small rockets and satellites. Tours of the site include a range control center, rocket launching facilities and an orientation movie.

Time: June-Aug., Mon.-Fri., by appt. only.

Place: 3.5 mi. E of US 13 on VA 175.

Contact: (804) 824-3411

National Wildlife Refuge

Whistling swans, three-foot high Sitka Deer, wild horses and 250 varieties of birds—including egrets, herons and ibises—frequent this natural wildlife wonderland. Swimming and surfing facilities are available in the area.

Place: Take Madox Blvd. to far end of town and cross bridge to the refuge on Assateague Island.

Contact: (804) 336-6122

Annual Pony Penning

Once a year, as part of a volunteer fireman's carnival, Chincoteague ponies are herded into the Assateague channel for a short swim to Chincoteague, where they are auctioned on the carnival

grounds. (The event was the basis for the children's classic, *Misty of Chincoteague*.) The mares and stallions not purchased are released to swim back to their island refuge.

Time: Pony swims: last week of July, in the morning, depending on the tide. Carnival: late July-early Aug., Mon.-Sat., 7:30 a.m.-noon.

Contact: President, Chincoteague Volunteer Fire Department, Chincoteague, VA 23336; Chamber of Commerce, (804) 336-6161.

Danville

Harvest Jubilee

This celebration of Danville's Victorian history is held in late September in the city's warehouse district. Victorian-style vendors, artists and craftsmen line the streets, peddling wares and vittles. Tours are conducted of Danville's Victorian homes and the National Tobacco Textile Museum. Victorian music, a parade of years, and antique displays are also featured.

Time: 2nd weekend in Sept.

Contact: Harvest Jubilee, Chairperson, P.O. Box 3300, Danville, VA 24541; (804) 799-5200.

VIRGINIA

Fort Belvoir

US Army Engineer Museum

Exhibits in this interesting museum trace the 200-year history of the US Army Corps of Engineers. Also on display are a map of the 1781 Battle of Yorktown, engineering models, presidential letters, paintings and flags.

Time: Mon.-Fri., 8 a.m.-4:30 p.m., Sat., 1-4 p.m.
Place: 16th and Belvoir Rd.
Contact: (202) 664-6104

Fort Lee

US Army Quartermaster Museum

One of the nation's finest military museums, it includes an arsenal of battle weapons, arrays of uniforms and decorations dating from 1775, and a century-old saddlemaker shop.

Time: Mon.-Fri., 8 a.m.-5 p.m.; Sat., Sun. and holidays, 11 a.m.-5 p.m.
Place: 2 mi. E of Petersburg.
Contact: US Army Quartermaster Museum, Fort Lee, VA 23801; (804) 734-4203.

Fredericksburg

Union Headquarters

This 18th-century mansion, Chatham Manor, served as a hospital during the Civil War. Union soldiers stayed here before crossing the river to fight the Battle of Fredericksburg. Today it boasts of beautiful rose gardens and a collection of Civil War memorabilia.

Time: 9 a.m.-5 p.m.
Place: 1 mi. E of town off VA 218.
Contact: (703) 373-9400

A Dog Day Afternoon

One day each year, Fredericksburg literally "goes to the dogs," as the Dog Mart, a 283-year-old celebration, fills the streets of the city. Highlights of the day include a dog auction; contests for the ugliest, best-dressed and funniest dogs; and a canine parade. For variety, the festival also includes band and fiddle music, Indian dancing, turkey- and hog-calling contests and foxhorn blowing.

Time: 1st Sat. in Oct.
Place: Downtown Fredericksburg.
Contact: (703) 373-1776

National Military Park

The Chancellorsville battlefield is one of four major Civil War battlefields in the Fredericksburg and Spotsylvania National Military Park. The Battles of Chancellorsville and Salem Church, fought here May 1-6, 1863, were among the most important engagements of the Civil War. Two visitor center museums feature exhibits and a documentary film. Special summer programs interpret military life and other Civil War themes.

Time: 9 a.m.-5 p.m.
Place: Lafayette Blvd. (US 1) and Sunlen Rd.
Contact: Fredericksburg and Spotslvania National Military Park, Fredericksburg, VA 22401; P.O. Box 679; (703) 373-4461

Hampton

Army Transportation Museum

The US Army Transportation Museum at Fort Eustis features an exhibit of the historical progress of military transportation since the revolutionary war, including a captive "flying saucer."

Time: Mon.-Fri., 8 a.m.-5 p.m.; Sun., noon-5 p.m.
Contact: P.O. Drawer D, Fort Eustis, VA 23604; (804) 878-3603.

Moon Rocks and More

Langley Air Force Base is headquarters for the Tactical Air Command and the laboratories of the NASA Langely Research Center and Visitor Center. Among the special attractions at the Visitor Center are exhibits of moon rock, a space suit, the Apollo 12 Command Module and other examples of aeronautics and space research. Movies are also shown.

Time: Mon.-Sat., 8:30 a.m.-4:30 p.m.; Sun., noon-4:30 p.m.
Contact: Langley Research Center, Hampton, VA 23665; (804) 827-2855.

Bluebird Gap Farm

Children can pet the farm animals here, and can view various fowl, farm machinery and a barn. Contains picnic and play areas.

Time: Wed.-Sun., 9 a.m.-5 p.m.
Place: On Pine Chapel Rd. between I-64 and Queen St.
Contact: (804) 727-6347

Hardy

Booker T. Washington National Monument

Embracing 224 acres, this monument is a partial recreation of the tobacco plantation on which Booker T. Washington was born as a slave. A visitor center features exhibits and a movie on Washington's life. Living history demonstrations are presented by costumed interpreters and farm animals of the 1860s can be seen from the self-guiding trail. Have a picnic on the grounds.

Time: Visitor center: 8:30 a.m.-5 p.m. Living history: mid-June-Labor Day, 8:30 a.m.-5 p.m.
Place: 20 mi. SE of Roanoke via VA 116 S to Burnt Chimney, then VA 122.
Contact: Rt. 1, Box 195, Hardy, VA 24101; (703) 721-2094.

Hopewell

Beautiful Wayside

CBS television newsman Charles Kuralt once called these gardens "America's most beautiful wayside." Created and privately maintained by the late Walter H. Misenheimer in a natural wooded setting, the gardens and boxwood-lined trails display colorful glimpses of dogwood, camellias, azaleas and delicate wild flowers.

Time: Best in azalea season, mid- to late-Apr.
Place: VA 10, 21 mi. E of Hopewell.

Contact: Mac Eubank, (804) 458-5536.
Note: Mr. Misenheimer tried unsuccessfully to deed his wayside to the State of Virginia, but the gift was declined and thus remains private property. Please leave it as you find it.

Keswick

The Blessing of the Hounds

Ever since 1928, the Blessing of the Hounds service has been held at Grace Church on Thanksgiving Day. The Keswick Hunt Club and members of other hunt clubs participate. The service is held outdoors where the horses, dogs and uniformed riders gather for blessings before they start the hunt, usually on a farm adjacent to church property.

Contact: Grace Episcopal Church, Box 43, Keswick, VA 22947; (804) 293-3549

Lexington

Steele's Tavern

The Cyrus McCormick Memorial Museum and Wayside in the village of Steele's Tavern is a shrine to the American inventor Cyrus McCormick. More than a dozen miniature model

VIRGINIA

Lexington

reapers, threshers, and bellows as well as a restored blacksmith shop, gristmill and slave quarters are on display. The farm and workshop where McCormick invented the reaper that revolutionized the world's agriculture is nearby. Picnic facilities are available.
Time: Mid-Apr.-mid-Oct., 8 a.m.-5 p.m. Rest of year, by appt.
Place: 20 mi. N of town on US 11.
Contact: (804) 377-2255

Lee's Chapel

Built in 1867 under the supervision of Robert E. Lee, the Lee Chapel and Museum sits on the campus of Washington and Lee University, where Lee served as president. It contains Lee's office and family crypt, a statue of Lee, and the famous Custis Family Portrait Collection. The shrine is a National Historic Landmark.
Time: Mid-Oct.-mid-Apr., Mon.-Sat., 9 a.m.-4 p.m.; Sun., 2-5 p.m. Mid-Apr.-mid-Oct., Mon.-Sat., 9 a.m.-5 p.m.; Sun., 2-5 p.m.
Place: On the campus of Washington and Lee University near Jefferson and Washington Sts.
Contact: (703) 463-9111, ext. 289

Virginia Military Institute

Known as "the West Point of the South," VMI was founded in 1839 and is the oldest state-supported military college in the nation. Stonewall Jackson taught here and General George C. Marshall was a 1901 graduate. Officially designated a National Historic District, VMI houses a museum containing Stonewall Jackson and George S. Patton mementos, a planetarium and the George Marshall Research Library.
Time: Mon.-Fri., 9 a.m.-4:30 p.m.; Sat., 9 a.m.-noon and 2-5 p.m.; Sun., 2-5 p.m.
Place: Museum: Jackson Memorial Hall.
Contact: Virginia Military Institute, Lexington, VA 24450; (703) 463-6232.

Dress Parade

Every Tuesday and Friday at 4:20 p.m. during fall and spring semesters, cadets of Virginia Military Institute march in full-dress parade. Guard mounts are conducted at 12:30 p.m. on those days.
Contact: (703) 463-6232

Goshen Pass

This breathtaking mountain gorge, formed by the Maury River, is ideal for picnicking, swimming, sightseeing or quiet relaxation.
Place: 15 mi. NE of Lexington via US 11 and VA 39.

Historic Walking Tour

Robert E. Lee's office, Stonewall Jackson's home and George C. Marshall's Nobel Peace Prize are among the highlights you'll see during a two-hour guided walking tour of historic Lexington. Take your pick of three self-guided tours: the Lee-Jackson Walking Tour, the VMI-Marshall Tour, and the Residential Tour. Excellent free brochures are provided.
Time: Tours: Apr. 1-Oct. 31, Mon.-Sat., 10 a.m.; Sun., 2 p.m.
Contact: Historic Lexington Visitor Center, Sloan House, 107 E. Washington St., Lexington, VA 24450; (703) 463-3777.

George C. Marshall Museum

Located on the west edge of the Virginia Military Institute Parade Ground, this museum traces Marshall's career, with particular emphasis on the years of the two world wars and the Marshall Plan. An audio-visual presentation traces the developments of World War II.

Time: Apr. 16-Oct. 14, Mon-Sat., 10 a.m.-4 p.m.; Sun., 2-5 p.m. Rest of year, Mon.-Sat., 10 a.m.-4 p.m.; Sun., 2-5 p.m.

Contact: Virginia Military Institute, P.O. Box 920, Lexington, VA 24450; (703) 463-7103.

Luray

Singing Tower

Situated in a beautiful park and garden, Luray Carillon Tower is 117 feet tall, 25 feet square at the base and contains 47 bells, the largest of which weighs 7,640 pounds. Regular concert recitals by famed Carillonneurs are best heard from a distance of 200-300 yards.

Time: Recitals: June 1-Sept. 14, Tues., Thurs., Sat. and Sun., 8 p.m.; Mar. 1-May 31 and Sept. 16-Oct. 30, 2 p.m. Additional recitals on Easter and Labor Day.

Place: 1 mi. W of town on US 211 at entrance to Luray Caverns.

Manassas

Bull Run Battle Site

Two great Civil War battles, the First and Second Battles of Manassas, also known as the two Battles of Bull Run, were fought here. The national Battlefield Park Visitor Center offers a museum and slide show program, and a three-dimensional map presents strategies of both battles. Also of interest is the Stone House, renovated as a Civil War field hospital.

Time: Grounds: 9 a.m.-dark. Visitor Center: Summer, 9 a.m.-6 p.m.; rest of year, 9 a.m.-5:30 p.m. The Stone House: June 15-Labor Day, 10 a.m.-5 p.m.

Place: On VA 234 near jct. of US 29/211.

Contact: Manassas National Battlefield Park, P.O. Box 1830, Manassas, VA 22110; (703) 754-7107.

McLean

Turkey Run Farm

This 100-acre farm and the hand-built cabin on its premises depict the daily life of a small family of the 1770s. Special evening programs feature country dances as well as 18th-century music and games.

Time: Apr. 1-Nov. 30, Wed.-Sun., 10 a.m.-4:30 p.m.; rest of year, Fri.-Sun., 10 a.m.-4:30 p.m. Evening programs: Apr.-Sept., second Thurs. of month.

Place: Exit 13 off I-495, then 2.25 mi. E on VA 193. Turn left and follow signs.

Contact: (703) 557-1356

Middleburg

Meredyth Vineyards

Individuals and groups are invited to tour this winery located in the historic foothills of the Bull Run Mountains, 90 minutes away from the nation's capital. The 30-minute guided tour culminates in a tasting session.

Contact: P.O. Box 347, Middleburg, VA 22117; (703) 687-6612.

Norfolk

Chrysler Museum

The Chrysler Museum's collection is one of the most important and comprehensive art assemblages in the US. Art treasures from every period of civilization and by virtually all of the masters of fine and decorative arts are on display. The museum's glass collection is one of the finest in the world. Visitors will want to browse through the gift shop and enjoy performing arts in the theater.

Time: Tues.-Sat., 10 a.m.-4 p.m.; Sun., 1-5 p.m.

Place: 3 blocks W of Olney Rd. and Virginia Beach Blvd.

Contact: (703) 622-1211

VIRGINIA

Norfolk

MacArthur Memorial

Housed in a city courthouse built in 1847, the MacArthur Memorial contains an extensive collection of exhibits and memorabilia tracing General Douglas MacArthur's controversial life and military career. There are nine galleries of displays that include the general's famous corncob pipe, the surrender documents that ended World War II, his 1950 staff car and a reconstruction of two of his offices. A continuous 22-minute film shows highlights of his life.

Time: Mon.-Sat., 10 a.m.-5 p.m.; Sun., 11 a.m.-5 p.m.
Place: City Hall Ave.
Contact: (804) 441-2382

Azalea Festival

Some 250,000 azaleas line 12 miles of paths in Norfolk during the annual International Azalea Festival held in late April. Norfolk's yearly salute to the North Atlantic Treaty Organization, the celebration combines dance, art and athletic tournaments into a week-long event that culminates with the Grand Parade through downtown and the queen's coronation in the beautiful Gardens by the Sea.

Time: Late April.
Contact: Norfolk Chamber of Commerce, 420 Bank St., Norfolk, VA 23501; (804) 622-2312.

St. Paul's Church

Built in 1739, St. Paul's Church was the lone survivor of the British bombardment of

Norfolk in 1776. A cannonball fired during that battle is still embedded in the southeastern wall of the church. Traditional services are still held here.

Time: Tues.-Sat., 10 a.m.-4 p.m.; Sun., 2-4 p.m. Services: Sun., 8 and 11 a.m.
Contact: (703) 627-4353

Harborfest

Tall ships, fireworks, roaring cannons and shouting pirates signal the celebration of Norfolk's annual Harborfest weekend each spring. The three-day waterfront festival features a variety of aquatic events and is climaxed by a Pirate's Ball at the Norfolk Boatbuilding School.

Time: Late May.
Contact: Norfolk Convention and Visitors Bureau, P.O. Box 238, Scope Plaza, Norfolk, VA 23501; (804) 441-5266.
Note: There is a nominal admission fee to the Pirate's Ball.

Petersburg

Siege Museum

A stunning Greek Revival structure, originally built as a tobacco and merchandise exchange, now houses the Siege Museum. Inside, displays and vivid audio-visual presentations depict conditions during the 10-month Civil War siege of Petersburg, the longest such siege in American history.

Time: Mon.-Sat., 9 a.m.-5 p.m.; Sun., 1-5 p.m.
Place: 15 W. Bank St.
Contact: Siege Museum, 15 W. Bank St., Petersburg, VA. 23803; (804) 861-2904.

Trapezium House

One of the most unique houses in Petersburg, this architectural oddity was built around 1817 by an eccentric Irish bachelor, Charles O'Hara. The story goes that O'Hara was convinced by a West Indian servant that a house with right angles would harbor evil spirits, so he ordered his home built in the form of a trapezoid, or trapezium—with no parallel sides and no right angles. A restoration of the house is soon to be completed.

Time: Mon.-Sat., 9 a.m.-5 p.m.; Sun., 1-5 p.m. Open as restoration permits.
Place: 244 Market St.
Contact: (804) 861-8080

Historic Mansion

Civil War relics abound in the Centre Hill Mansion Museum in Petersburg. On display are such items as General Grant's furniture and wagons used by General Sherman on his march through Georgia. Elegant federal chandeliers and mid-19th-century music recreate the ambience of the period.

Time: Mon.-Sat., 9 a.m.-5 p.m.; Sun., 1-5 p.m.
Place: Centre Hill Court, off Franklin St.
Contact: (804) 732-8081

Tobacco Plant Tour

You'll see the whole story of tobacco—from seed to smoke —during a tour of the Brown and Williamson Tobacco Corporation. A highlight of the tour is the chance to watch whirring machines swallow tobacco and paper and spit out cigarettes in split-seconds. Also offered is an audio-visual presentation on the cultivation of the crop.

Time: Mon.-Fri., 8:30 a.m.-4 p.m.
Place: 325 Brown St.
Contact: (804) 732-5222, ext. 232
Note: Tours are for individuals and groups of 15 visitors or less. Larger groups may arrange tours by calling in advance.

Farmers Bank

Memories of the antebellum days of finance and trade come to life in one of the oldest known bank buildings in America. See and hear an audio-visual account of early American banking inside the old double vault. Witness the actual press and plates once used to print the bank's own brand of money.

Time: Mon.-Sat., 9 a.m.-5 p.m.; Sun., 1-5 p.m.
Place: 19 Bollingbrook St., at Cockade Alley.
Contact: (804) 861-1590

National Battlefield

This 1,531-acre park has been established to commemorate the ten-month Siege of Petersburg during the Civil War, the longest siege any American city has ever endured. Touring this historic area, you'll see and hear a complete account of the Siege, view the site of the famous Battle of the Crater, and come upon other points of interest, including a museum of battlefield weapons and uniforms. Every summer, local college students don Blue and Gray outfits to recreate 1860s life on this battlefield.

Time: Mid-June-Labor Day, 8 a.m.-7 p.m.; rest of year, 8 a.m.-5 p.m.
Place: E of town on VA 36.
Contact: Petersburg National Battlefield, P.O. Box 549, Petersburg, VA 23803; (804) 732-3531.

Church Tiffany Windows

One of America's most beautiful art treasures is housed in the Old Blandford Church in Petersburg. The church is the only building in America to have had its every window—15 in all—designed by Louis C. Tiffany, the master of Art Nouveau. Originally built in 1734,

VIRGINIA

Petersburg

the church was restored as a Confederate shrine in 1901.
Time: Mon.-Sat., 9 a.m.-5 p.m.; Sun., noon-5 p.m.
Place: 319 S. Crater Rd.
Contact: (804) 732-2230

Quartermaster Museum

From revolutionary war canteens to General George Patton's jeep, this unusual museum contains a variety of items associated with the Quartermaster Corps that has fed, housed, clothed and supplied American troops for almost 200 years.
Time: Mon.-Fri., 8 a.m.-5 p.m.; Sat., Sun., 1-5 p.m.
Place: Fort Lee, on VA 36.
Contact: (804) 734-1854

Portsmouth

Lightship Museum

This Coast Guard museum is built into an actual lightship. Exhibits include Coast Guard equipment and realistically fitted quarters of the officers and crew, as well as historic artifacts of Coast Guard lightships of the past century.
Time: Tues.-Sat., 10 a.m.-4:45 p.m.; Sun., 2-4:45 p.m.
Place: London Slip at Water St.

Contact: Lightship Museum, London Slip at Water St., Portsmouth, VA 23704; (804) 393-8741.

Naval History Museum

Located on the Elizabeth River waterfront, the Portsmouth Naval Shipyard Museum displays numerous ship models, uniforms and historic flags. Special attractions are the original *Merrimac* and a Polaris missile.
Time: Tues.-Sat., 10 a.m.-5 p.m.; Sun., 2-5 p.m.
Place: 2 High St.
Contact: Portsmouth Naval Shipyard Museum, P.O. Box 248, 2 High St., Portsmouth, VA 23705; (804) 393-8591.

Richmond

Confederate Capital

This National Battlefield Park commemorates those battles waged to defend the confederate capital. Landmarks from the famous Battle of Cold Harbor and other historic Civil War confrontations are preserved and maintained here. Offers an audio-visual program and exhibits on battles in the Richmond area. See also the exhibits in the Fort Harrison Visitor Center.
Time: Park: 8:30 a.m.-5 p.m. Visitor center and headquar-

ters: 9 a.m.-5 p.m. Fort Harrison Visitor Center: June-Aug., 9:30 a.m.-5:30 p.m.; Apr.-May and Sept.-Oct., Sat.-Sun. only.
Place: 3215 E. Broad St.
Contact: (804) 795-1115

Dogwood Dell Amphitheater

Free ballet, opera and musical plays are held on summer evenings at this lake-studded sanctuary. Carillon concerts chime forth daily. Seats about 2,000.
Place: Byrd Park.
Contact: (804) 780-8686

Maymont Park

This 105-acre, turn-of-the-century estate features a Nature Center, a Victorian-Edwardian museum house, Japanese and Italian gardens and domestic and wild animal exhibits. Children will love the family of bears.
Time: Park: Apr.-Oct., 10 a.m.-7 p.m.; Nov.-Mar., 10 a.m.-5 p.m. Exhibits: Apr.-Oct., Tues.-Sat., 11 a.m.-5 p.m.; Sun., noon-6 p.m. Nov.-Mar., Tues.-Sun., noon-4:30 p.m.
Place: Hampton St. and Pennsylvania Ave.
Contact: 1700 Hampton St., Richmond, VA 23220; (804) 358-7166.

St. John's Church

This quaint frame church was built in 1741 and is the site of

Patrick Henry's famous "Give me liberty . . ." speech which ignited the American Revolution. Reenactments of the speech can be heard on special occasions.

Time: Tours: Feb.-Nov., 10 a.m.-4 p.m. Services: Sun., 11 a.m.
Place: 25th at Broad St.
Contact: St. John's Episcopal Church, 25th at Broad St., Richmond, VA 23223; (804) 795-1300.
Note: Donations accepted. Off-hour tours for groups of 30 or more, 50 cents each.

Bejeweled Eggs

The Virginia Museum of Fine Arts contains galleries filled with everything from jeweled Russian Easter Eggs and Egyptian gold to Renaissance and Impressionist paintings.

Time: Tues.-Sat., 11 a.m.-5 p.m.; Sun., 1-5 p.m.
Place: Boulevard and Grove Aves.
Contact: (804) 257-0844

Restored Homes

More than 300 19th-century homes have been restored in this historic eight-block area called Church Hill—the oldest part of the city. The history of this area, which surrounds Old St. John's Church, includes an Indian massacre of an early English settlement.

Contact: (804) 358-5511

State Capitol

Designed by Thomas Jefferson, the Roman temple-like Virginia State Capitol is the first public example of neo-classical architecture and is the second oldest working capitol in the US. The legislators who meet here now represent the world's oldest English-speaking legislative body with an uninterrupted history. In the rotunda is a statue of George Washington, the only one he ever posed for.

Time: Apr. 1-Nov. 30, 9 a.m.-5 p.m.; rest of year, Mon.-Sat., 9 a.m.-5 p.m.; Sun., 1-5 p.m.
Place: Capitol Sq., 9th and Grace St.
Contact: The Capitol of Virginia, 9th and Grace St., Richmond, VA 23219; (804) 786-4344.

Roanoke

Scenic Drive

The Blue Ridge Parkway, a 469-mile scenic motorway, connects Shenandoah National Park in Virginia and the Great Smoky Mountains National Park in North Carolina and Tennessee. Following the crest of the Blue Ridge at heights from 649 to 6,053 feet, the road overlooks picturesque panoramas of the Southern Highlands. Among the most interesting sites are Humpback Rocks, James River Wayside, Peaks of Otter and Mabry Mill. Food, lodging and recreational facilities are available along the way.

Contact: Blue Ridge Pkwy., P.O. Box 1710, Roanoke, VA 24008; (703) 982-6213.
Note: Parkway is open all year but sections of the road may be closed in icy or snowy weather. The speed limit of 45 mph is strictly enforced. It is advisable to keep gas tanks at least half-filled.

VIRGINIA

Staunton

Summer Band Concerts

Gypsy Hill Park on Churchville Avenue is the site of summer band concerts every Monday night in Staunton. A special concert by the Statler Brothers is held on the Fourth of July.
Contact: (703) 886-8435

Virginia Beach

Psychic Research Center

A library containing 12,000 psychic readings of the mystic, Edgar Cayce, is the featured attraction at the Association for Research and Enlightenment in Virginia Beach. In addition, free lectures on the world of clairvoyance are presented every other Sunday afternoon at 3:30 in the fall, winter and spring. In summer, frequent lectures and experiments are open to the public.
Time: Library: 9 a.m.-5 p.m. Call ahead for lecture schedule. Center: Mon.-Sat., 9 a.m.-10 p.m.; Sun., 1-10 p.m.
Place: 67 Atlantic St.
Contact: (804) 428-3588

Native Lotus

The last substantial growth of rare native American lotus can be seen here in late July and early August. Seeds from these yellow-blossomed water plants have been sent as far away as Japan.
Place: Saudbridge, 10 mi. S of town.
Contact: (804) 425-7511

Oldest Lighthouse

The oldest lighthouse in the United States, dating back to 1791, can be found within the Fort Story Army Post next to the Cape Henry Memorial. Visitors' passes to enter Fort Story are issued at the East Gate, north end of Atlantic Avenue, or at the West Gate on US 60.
Contact: (804) 425-7511

Wakefield

Washington's Birthplace

On the south side of the Potomac River 38 miles from Fredericksburg is a reproduction of the plantation where George Washington was born. The 538-acre site, known as Wakefield, includes a monument built of old brick on the location of the original Washington home, which

burned in 1779. Many of the Washington family furnishings are among the 18th-century antiques in the memorial mansion. Outside, the Colonial Living Farm recreates farm scenes of Washington's boyhood.
Time: 9 a.m.-5 p.m.
Place: 38 mi. E of Fredericksburg off VA 3.
Contact: (804) 224-0196

Williamsburg

Anheuser Busch Hospitality Center

During a visit to the Anheuser Busch Hospitality Center, you can see a color film about the brewery's famous Clydesdale horses and the history of beer. Or you can tour a gallery of Williamsburg area archaeological treasures, stroll through a sunlit courtyard, or peruse the gift shop.
Time: 9 a.m.-4 p.m.
Place: 5 mi. E of Williamsburg on VA 60; then follow the signs to the parking lot.
Contact: (804) 253-3036

Walking Tour

Take a free walk around historic Williamsburg and follow the footsteps of American history. Among the attractions awaiting you en route are the Wren Building, the oldest

VIRGINIA

continuously used structure in the US, a courthouse built in 1770, picturesque William and Mary College and the Abby Aldrich Rockefeller Art Museum. It's a hike well worth the effort.
Contact: (804) 229-1000

Large Folk Art Collection

The Abby Aldrich Rockefeller Folk Art Center offers the largest collection of American primitive paintings and other art objects in the U.S.—some 1,300 in all. Presented to colonial Williamsburg by Mrs. John D. Rockefeller, Jr., the center is housed in a 19th-century building next to the Williamsburg Inn.
Time: Apr.-Dec., noon-8 p.m.; Jan.-Mar., noon-6 p.m.
Place: 307 S. England St.
Contact: (804) 229-1000, ext. 2424

Yorktown

Yorktown Battlefield

The Colonial National Historical Park, overlooking the historic York River, offers a self-guided tour through the battle fields where the British Army surrendered to George Washington's troops on Oct. 19, 1781. You'll pass fighting lines and historic houses. A muse-

um in the Visitor Center contains exhibits and audio-visual presentations.
Time: 8:30 a.m.-sunset.
Place: 1.5 mi. S of town at the end of Colonial Pkwy.
Contact: Colonial National Historical Park, P.O. Box 210, Yorktown, VA 23690; (804) 898-3400.

Celebrate Yorktown

The surrender of the British at the Battle of Yorktown will be celebrated throughout this town at city parks, historic homes and restored battlefields. Call the contact for details on events, which include art exhibits, theatrical presentations, military and waterfront events, fireworks, entertainment, guest speakers and battle reenactments.
Contact: (804) 898-7229

Statewide

Beaches

Along the Atlantic Coast, Virginia is flanked by beaches with fine sand and tidewater that is just right for swimming, surfing and fishing. Two of these are free to visitors — Virginia Beach and Ocean View in Norfolk. Virginia Beach is a narrow strip of sand noted for its resort hotel and popular

night spots as well as for its beach-related activity.
Contact: (804) 786-4484
Note: Salt-water fishing is free from the numerous public beaches.

INDEX

ATTRACTIONS·THE BEST FREE
THE BEST FREE ATTRACTIONS·
FREE ATTRACTIONS·THE BEST
ATTRACTIONS·THE BEST FREE
THE BEST FREE ATTRACTIONS·
FREE ATTRACTIONS·THE BEST
ATTRACTIONS·THE BEST FREE
THE BEST FREE ATTRACTIONS·
ATTRACTIONS·THE BEST FREE
THE BEST FREE ATTRACTIONS·
FREE ATTRACTIONS·THE BEST
ATTRACTIONS·THE BEST FREE
THE BEST FREE ATTRACTIONS·

INDEX

A

Agriculture, see Farming
Aircraft: Ala., 81; Fla., 21, 28; Miss., 58; N.C., 72; Tex., 124
Alabama, 3-10
Animals, see Birds; Refuges, wildlife; Wildlife; Zoos
Antebellum homes: Ala., 4, 6, 8, 9; Ark., 14; Ga., 36, 43, 44; La., 48, 49; Miss., 60, 61; S.C., 96; Tex., 121, 125
Antiques: Ala., 8, 10; Ga., 43; La., 52; S.C., 96; Tenn., 107; Va., 131. *See also* Automobiles, antique
Aquaria: Ala., 5; La., 51; N.C., 72; S.C., 99; Tenn., 109; Tex., 116, 123
Arboreta: Ala., 4; La., 55
Archaeological sites, ruins and artifacts: Ala., 5; Fla., 23; Miss., 61; Okla., 80, 83, 85, 88; Tenn., 108
Architectural attractions: Ala., 6, 8, 10; Ark., 14; Ga., 37, 38, 40, 43; La., 46, 52; Miss., 60; N.C., 69, 77; Okla., 83, 86, 90; S.C., 96; Tenn., 104, 107, 110; Tex., 124; Va., 129, 130, 136-139. *See also* Antebellum homes
Arkansas, 11-17
Arts and crafts: Ala., 7; Ark., 12, 13; Fla., 26, 27, 30; Ga., 42; La., 48; Miss., 63; N.C., 66, 67, 72, 77; Okla., 81, 82, 88; S.C., 95; Va., 130, 131, 141. *See also* Fine arts; Museums, fine art
Astronomy clubs: Ga., 36. *See also* Observatories, Planetaria
Auctions: Fla., 20, 25, 33; N.C., 77; S.C., 97; Tenn., 111; Tex., 114, 123; Va., 132

Authors, see Literary sites
Automobiles, antique: Ala., 8; N.C., 67. *See also* Stock cars
Auto tours, see Drives, scenic
Aviaries: N.C., 78. *See also* Birds; Refuges, wildlife; Zoos

B

Backpacking, see Hiking
Ballet: Tenn., 107; Tex., 116, 120, 121; Va., 138. *See also* Dancing, Fine arts
Balloons, hot air: Ark., 13, 14
Bands, see Concerts
Banks: Va., 137
Banjo picking: Ark., 15. *See also* Concerts, Fiddling
Battle sites: Ala., 5, 7; Ark., 15, 16; Ga., 41, 42; La., 48; Miss., 63; N.C., 68, 71, 73; Okla., 81; Tenn., 104, 105, 109, 111; Tex., 119, 124; Va., 132, 137, 138, 141
Beachcombing: Fla., 31
Beaches: Ala., 10; Fla., 21, 24, 33, 34; La., 49, 50; Miss., 58; N.C., 68, 73; S.C., 94, 99; Va., 141. *See also* Coastlines, Lakes
Beer, see Breweries
Bells, see Carillon chimes
Berry picking: Tenn., 106
Biking: Fla., 24; Tenn., 112; Va., 129
Biological exhibits: La., 48; N.C., 69, 77
Birds: Ala., 4; Ark., 16; Fla., 24, 25, 26, 33; La., 49, 54; Miss., 58, 59; N.C., 70, 78; Okla., 81; S.C., 94, 99, 100; Tex., 114, 119, 123; Va., 131. *See also* Aviaries; Refuges, wildlife; Wildlife; Zoos

Boating: Ark., 12; Fla., 24, 32, 33; Ga., 38, 39, 41; La., 46; Miss., 59; N.C., 66; Okla., 90; Tenn., 104, 112; Tex., 117, 119. *See also* Whitewater
Boats, see Ships, Shrimp boats
Botanical gardens, see Arboreta, Flowers, Gardens, Plant life
Breweries: Fla., 31; Ga., 43; La., 51; N.C., 77; Tenn., 108; Tex., 124; Va., 140. *See also* Distilleries, Wineries
Bridges: Ala., 9; Miss., 62; S.C., 98; Va., 129
Bus rides: Fla., 32; Tenn., 105, 107

C

Camping: Fla., 23; Ga., 41; La., 46; Miss., 59, 62; N.C., 68; Okla., 81, 91; Tenn., 104, 110; Tex., 117
Canoeing, see Boating
Canyons: Ala., 6; N.C., 70; Tex., 122, 123. *See also* Gorges
Carillon chimes: Fla., 26; La., 51, 55; Va., 130, 135
Carnivals, see Festivals
Cars, see Automobiles, antique; Drives, scenic; Stock cars
Cattle, see Livestock
Caves: Ala., 5; Ark., 15, 17; Tex., 117
Celebrations, see Ceremonies, Festivals
Cemeteries: Ala., 5; Ga., 36, 37, 38; Miss., 62; N.C., 71; S.C., 97; Tenn., 104, 106; Va., 130
Ceremonies: Ala., 4, 9; Fla., 33; Ga., 39; Okla., 84; S.C., 97
Chapels, see Churches
Children's attractions: Ark., 14; Fla., 20, 28, 31; La., 52; Okla., 82, 85; S.C., 94; Tex., 120; Va., 129, 133, 138

INDEX

Forests, national: La., 46; Miss., 58, 59
Forts: Ala., 6; Ark., 12; Fla., 24; Ga., 43; La., 47; N.C., 73; Okla., 83; S.C., 94; Tenn., 105, 108; Tex., 118; Va., 128, 140. *See also* Historic sites
Fossils: Miss., 59; N.C., 70, 71; Okla., 85; Tex., 116, 121, 123
Fountains: Ala., 8

G

Galleries, see Fine art; Museums, fine art
Gardens: Ala., 4, 7, 10; Fla., 25-28, 31, 33; Ga., 41, 43, 44; La., 46, 50-52, 55; Miss., 58-60; N.C., 66, 67, 69, 75-77; Okla., 89; S.C., 98, 100; Tenn., 108; Tex., 114, 116, 118, 125, 126; Va., 133, 136, 140. *See also* Flowers, Plant life
Gems, see Minerals
Georgia, 35-44
Gold panning: Ga., 40
Gorges: N.C., 70, 73; Va., 134
Grave rubbings, see Rubbings, tombstone
Graveyards, see Cemeteries
Guns, see Firearms

H

Harbors: Fla., 22; Tex., 120
Hiking: Ala., 6; Ark., 12-15, 17; Fla., 24, 25, 27; Ga., 39; La., 46, 55; Miss., 58, 61-63; N.C., 66-68, 70, 73; Okla., 81, 89, 92; S.C., 99; Tenn., 104-106, 109, 112; Tex., 118; Va., 129, 133, 141. *See also* Walking tours
Historical societies: Okla., 86

Historic figures: Ala., 8, 10; Ark., 14; Fla., 20; La., 53; Miss., 63; N.C., 74, 75; Okla., 86; Tex., 114, 115, 121, 122. *See also* Famous people, Literary sites
Historic sites: Ala., 4, 7-10; Ark., 12-14; Fla., 20, 22, 24, 27-29, 32; Ga., 36-39, 42-44; La., 46-48, 52-54; Miss., 59, 60, 62, 63; N.C., 68, 71-75, 77; Okla., 80, 81, 85, 88, 90; S.C., 94-96, 97, 100, 101; Tenn., 104, 106, 107, 109; Tex., 115, 118, 121, 124; Va., 128-130, 139, 140
Historic trails: Ga., 40; Okla., 84, 91; Tenn., 104-106
Horses: Fla., 27, 28; La., 50; N.C., 74; S.C., 94; Tenn., 111; Va., 131, 133, 140
Hot springs, see Springs, hot
Hunting: La., 46. *See also* Snake hunts

I

Insects, see Wildlife
Introduction, 1
Inventions: Va., 133

J

Jogging: Tex., 119; Va., 129
Jousting: La., 56

L

Lakes: Ark., 12, 13; Ga., 39, 41; La., 50, 51, 55
Libraries: Miss., 60, 62; Okla., 83, 87; Tex., 114, 115, 120, 126; Va., 134, 140

Lighthouses: Fla., 24; N.C., 71; S.C., 94; Va., 129, 140
Literary sites: Ga., 38, 42; La., 54; Miss., 61, 62; N.C., 66, 70; Tex., 126; Va., 131
Livestock: Fla., 20, 25, 30; Okla., 87, 91; Tex., 114, 125. *See also* Farming, Ranching
Locks: Ala., 6. *See also* Dams
Logging: Tex., 122
Louisiana, 45-56

M

Manufacturers: Ala., 6; Ark., 16; Fla., 22, 25, 26, 30, 32; Ga., 39, 40, 43; La., 51, 53, 54; N.C., 72, 74, 76, 77; Okla., 83, 89; Tenn., 109; Tex., 115; Va., 137
Marine life: Ala., 5; Fla., 23, 24, 33; Miss., 58; N.C., 72, 73; Tex., 116
Maritime attractions: N.C., 68. *See also* Marine life, Ships
Markets: Fla., 29; Ga., 38; La., 52; Tex., 115, 124
Memorials: Okla., 82
Memorials, national: Fla., 20; N.C., 72; Tex., 117; Va., 130, 136
Memorials, state: N.C., 74; Va., 140
Military attractions: Ala., 5, 9; Ark., 15; Fla., 26; Ga., 36, 40, 41; La., 46, 48; Miss., 58, 60, 63; N.C., 70; Okla., 82, 84, 86, 87; S.C., 94-97, 99, 100; Tenn., 104, 111; Tex., 117, 124; Va., 129-132, 134, 136, 138, 141. *See also* Battle sites, Forts, Historic sites
Mills: N.C., 71; Tex., 123
Mills, sugar: Fla., 27, 29; La., 46; Tenn., 112
Minerals: Ala., 4; Ark., 14; Ga., 42; N.C., 66, 68, 70, 75; Okla., 81;

Response Page

We are eager to keep *The Best Free Attractions* as accurate and useful to travelers as possible. If you find any changes in times, contacts and so on, or any alterations in the nature of the attractions themselves, please note them on the form below and send them to us.

In addition, if you find any new free attractions that you'd like to see included in future revisions, you can use the form below to let us know about them.

Thanks for your help.

☐ Change in Free Attraction ☐ New Free Attraction

City: _____

Name of Attraction: _____

Description: _____

_____

_____

_____

Time: _____

Place: _____

Contact: _____

Note: _____

_____

Send to: **Meadowbrook Press** Dept. FRAT
18318 Minnetonka Blvd.
Deephaven, MN 55391

Response Page

☐ Change in Free Attraction   ☐ New Free Attraction

City: _____   Time: _____

Name of Attraction: _____   Place: _____

Description: _____   Contact: _____

_____   Note: _____

_____

_____   Send to: **Meadowbrook Press**   Dept. FRAT
                                        18318 Minnetonka Blvd.
                                        Deephaven, MN 55391

FREE STUFF BOOKS

FREE STUFF FOR KIDS
Over 250 of the best free and up-to-a-dollar
things kids can get by mail:
- coins & stamps
- bumper stickers & decals
- posters & maps
$3.75 ppd.

FREE STUFF FOR COOKS
Over 250 of the best free and up-to-a-dollar
booklets and samples cooks can get by
mail:
- cookbooks & recipe cards
- money-saving shopping guides
- seeds & spices
$3.75 ppd.

FREE STUFF FOR PARENTS
Over 250 of the best free and up-to-a-dollar
booklets and samples parents can get by
mail:
- sample teethers
- booklets on pregnancy & childbirth
- sample newsletters
$3.75 ppd.

FREE STUFF FOR HOME & GARDEN
Over 350 of the best free and up-to-a-dollar
booklets and samples homeowners and
gardeners can get by mail:
- booklets on home improvement & energy
- plans for do-it-yourself projects
- sample seeds
$3.75 ppd.

FREE STUFF FOR TRAVELERS
Over 1000 of the best free and
up-to-a-dollar publications and products
travelers can get by mail:
- guidebooks to cities, states & foreign
  countries
- pamphlets on attractions, festivals &
  parks
- posters, calendars & maps
$3.75 ppd.

Whitman's
THE BEST EUROPEAN TRAVEL TIPS
What the travel guides don't tell about
Europe: indispensible, easy-to-read tips
tell how to avoid tourist traps, rip-offs
and snafus...and have the most fun for
the money. **$5.75 ppd.**

THE BEST FREE ATTRACTIONS

THE BEST FREE ATTRACTIONS

THE BEST FREE ATTRACTIONS SOUTH

From North Carolina to Texas, it's a land swarming with surprises – and over 1,500 of them free:

- alligator and turtle stalking
- cow chip tosses & mule races
- free bluegrass, watermelon & barbecues!

THE BEST FREE ATTRACTIONS WEST

Just passing through from California to Montana? It's all free and there for the asking:

- belching volcanoes & miniature forests
- gold panning & quarter horse racing
- vineyard tours and free wine samples!

THE BEST FREE ATTRACTIONS EAST

Over 1,500 irresistible attractions – all free – from West Virginia to Maine (the proper east coast):

- a witchtrial courthouse with evidence
- aviaries where *you* are caged
- the "gentle giants" – and free beer!

THE BEST FREE ATTRACTIONS MIDWEST

From Kentucky to North Dakota, the Midwest is chock-full of free things:

- camel rides and shark feedings
- stagecoaches and magic tricks
- hobo conventions – with free Mulligan stew!

SOUTH
Alabama, Arkansas, Florida, Georgia, Louisiana, Mississippi, North Carolina, Oklahoma, South Carolina, Tennessee, Texas, Virginia

WEST
Alaska, Arizona, California, Colorado, Hawaii, Idaho, Montana, Nevada, New Mexico. Oregon, Utah, Washington, Wyoming

EAST
Connecticut, Delaware, DC, Maine, Maryland, Massachusetts, New Hampshire, New Jersey, New York, Pennsylvania, Rhode Island, Vermont, Virginia, West Virginia

MIDWEST
Illinois, Indiana, Iowa, Kansas, Kentucky, Michigan, Minnesota, Missouri, Nebraska, North Dakota, Ohio, South Dakota, Wisconsin

$4.75 ppd. each

BOOKS BY VICKI LANSKY

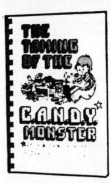

Hundreds of parent-tested ideas for the first five years. Includes topics such as baby care, feeding, self esteem and more. **Spiral bound. $5.75 ppd.**

The most popular baby book and tot food cookbook for new parents. Includes over 200 recipes and ideas. **Spiral bound. $5.75 ppd.**

The classic cookbook that helps you get your children to eat less sugary, salty junk food...and like it! **Spiral bound. $5.75 ppd.**

ORDER FORM

BOOKS (Prices include postage and handling.)

_____ BEST BABY NAME BOOK ..... $3.75 ppd.
_____ BEST FREE ATTRACTIONS (EAST) .... $4.75 ppd.
_____ BEST FREE ATTRACTIONS (MIDWEST) .... $4.75 ppd.
_____ BEST FREE ATTRACTIONS (SOUTH) .... $4.75 ppd.
_____ BEST FREE ATTRACTIONS (WEST) .... $4.75 ppd.
_____ BEST EUROPEAN TRAVEL TIPS $5.75 ppd.
_____ FREE STUFF FOR TRAVELERS .... $3.75 ppd.

_____ FREE STUFF FOR COOKS ..... $3.75 ppd.
_____ FREE STUFF FOR HOME AND GARDEN .... $3.75 ppd.
_____ FREE STUFF FOR KIDS .... $3.75 ppd.
_____ FREE STUFF FOR PARENTS ... $3.75 ppd.
_____ BEST PRACTICAL PARENTING TIPS .... $5.75 ppd.
_____ FEED ME I'M YOURS .... $5.75 ppd.
_____ TAMING THE CANDY MONSTER $5.75 ppd.

If ordering more than six books, please write to us for quantity discount rates.

$ _____ total enclosed

Make checks payable to:
Meadowbrook Press Dept. FA-S DM
18318 Minnetonka Boulevard
Deephaven, Minnesota 55391

Name: _____

Address: _____

_____ Zip _____